Lessons From the Best Coach

JAY MARTIN

Foreword by Anson Dorrance

LESSONS FROM THE BEST COACH

DEVELOP A WINNING TEAM CULTURE THAT LASTS

Meyer & Meyer Sport

British Library of Cataloguing in Publication Data
A catalogue record for this book is available from the British Library

Lessons From the Best Coach
Maidenhead: Meyer & Meyer Sport (UK) Ltd., 2024
ISBN: 978-1-78255-263-5

Aachen, Auckland, Beirut, Cairo, Cape Town, Dubai, Hägendorf, Hong Kong, Indianapolis, Maidenhead, Manila, New Delhi, Singapore, Sydney, Tehran, Vienna

Member of the World Sport Publishers' Association (WSPA), www.w-s-p-a.org

Printed by Integrated Books International
Printed in the United States of America
ISBN: 978-1-78255-263-5
Email: info@m-m-sports.com
www.thesportspublisher.com

CONTENTS

FOREWORD

Yesterday, I read *Lessons From the Best Coach*. I did it in one sitting. I have never done that before with any book, but it was worth the investment of my time to read something with a roadmap so practical, so empowering, by a man with an extraordinary track record that *all of us* can learn from.

I love the debates we coaches have about player development, leadership, and culture. Years ago, I was invited to be a speaker for the organization, "What Drives Winning." I remember one discussion about the evolution of elite coaching, and I was skeptical, especially when I was a young, ambitious coach, about the character development piece that was at its core. When I started coaching collegiately as a 24-year-old, it was only about the Xs and Os, running a good practice, and wanting to build my confidence as a coach. Of course, by the time they brought me in to speak, I was older, completely sold on character development, and the title of my talk for them was "Grading Character." But I had not started there. I had evolved into that kind of coach. So where are you in your coaching evolution? Are you ready for the next step?

What I like about the overwhelming theme of Jay Martin's book is not so much what you are teaching in the one-and-a-half to two hours you are training, but what happens in your soccer program for the other twenty-two hours. Because this is a *coaching* book, not a *soccer coaching* book. But how do you get to an environment that will be embraced by the team members? Trust me, if you want success, your environment must be embraced by everyone in your culture. And speaking of culture, how do you create it? I have never read anything with such a specific road map to construct culture as this book.

Jay Martin's insights are taking us into another brave new world in which "coaches don't develop players; only players make players better." Our culture right now is "coach centric," and we must change it to "player centric" to catch up to the social changes and the changes in the people we are coaching. There is a sea of change in the modern coaching world from "telling players what to do" to "asking questions," to see what they know to be able to instruct them better and help them improve faster. This route is harder because you must win the trust of your players. And to accelerate players' growth, let them create the team's "Core Values." Jay Martin lets the players own and run as much as possible with his light hand on the tiller because unlike many sports, our sport requires athletes make decisions on the field without the coach, so athletes must organize outside the lines as leaders as well.

One of the biggest challenges in coaching today is getting an athlete's personal narrative to the truth because that narrative is designed to protect the athlete from pain and accountability, but sometimes (the data tells us 85% of the time), it is a false narrative. The detail that this book provides to frame and inspire growth makes it clear why Jay Martin has had so much extraordinary and long-term success.

When I was young, I read two books that had a profound effect on my thinking and ambition. They were Jim Collins' books, *Built to Last* and *Good to Great*. I wanted to be that "Level 5 Leader" that, according to Collins, has seemingly come from Mars and is self-effacing, quiet, reserved ... a paradoxical blend of personal humility and professional will. I failed. Dr. Jay Martin did not. He is that leader from Mars. His hand on the tiller is light, but don't be fooled, when the hurricane hits (and in *every* season a hurricane will hit), his grip will tighten and the hard decisions will be made, taking the team in the right direction. When you read this book, you will see why the amazing culture of Ohio Wesleyan is so successful, and like me, you will be stealing practical ideas and philosophies that will impact the human development of the people you lead. And honestly human development is the higher calling.

–Anson Dorrance
Head women's soccer coach, University of North Carolina

PREFACE

On Friday December 2, 2011, the Ohio Wesleyan University soccer team was playing in the national Division III semi-final in San Antonio, Texas. The opponent was Montclair State University, New Jersey, who won the New Jersey Collegiate Association championship with a 19-2-0 record. In the stands, there were 78 former OWU players. They knew none of the members on the current team. They were there to support the program. A program they contributed to when they were students at OWU!

They came to San Antonio on their own. They paid their own way down to Texas and took valuable time away from their families during the holiday season.

The OWU team won the game 4-0. On Saturday December 3, 2011, an additional 48 former players flew into San Antonio. They were there to support the program. There were even parents of former players in San Antonio!

There were so many former OWU players that there was an impromptu alumni game at Trinity University hosted by the TU coach and good friend Paul McGinlay!

In the final game, OWU defeated a very good Calvin College team 2-1 to win their second national championship. The stands were across the field from the team benches. When the whistle blew, all the OWU players ran across the field and jumped into the stands to celebrate with the former players. See the photo. Let me repeat that none of the alumni knew any of the current players, but they knew the program.

As I watched the celebration, my wife, JoAnn, came up to me and said, "Jay, this is what you do and it has very little to do with soccer! You have connected with these players for the last 35 years. Different players, different generations, the same connection."

I knew that we had a good program. I can read. I knew we won a lot of games. But this was a realization. The program was more important than soccer for these players and former players.

I knew that the OWU men's soccer program meant more to the players than just playing a soccer game. It made a lasting impact. How can you create that with your team, whether in sports or business?

This is what this book is about. How can you, as a coach, a manager, or a leader, create an environment that empowers your players or workers or followers? In this book, coach and manager and leader are interchangeable. The coach is in a leadership position. Is he or she a leader? The manager is a coach and in a leadership position—or are they? The leader is the pinnacle.

Coaching or management and leadership is changing. The "*my-way-or-the-highway mentality*" is no longer appropriate. The players or employees today want more. Good coaches, managers, or leaders want to create an environment that empowers the players/employees/followers. They want to create an environment that is positive. They want to create an environment where there is a connection between the coach or manager and the players and followers. The best teams and organizations create an emotional attachment between the players or followers and the organization. I want my players to look at the soccer program as more important than a team.

To me, a soccer team is the 2 hours each day at practice; a soccer program is the other 22 hours. How many teams have you been on that were 2 hours each day without the other 22 hours? My guess is most of them!

Team dynamics suggest that a team goes through four stages. The first stage is the "forming" stage. The second phase is the "storming" stage. The third stage is the "norming" stage," and finally, the "performing" stage. I contend that most teams never get past the storming stage. This book will lead you and your team or organization through the storming stage and into the performing stage.

This book will examine the ways a coach, manager, or leader can create an environment that will be embraced by the team members. It will present an environment that is conducive to intrinsic motivation. All good organizations thrive on intrinsic motivation!

This book explains how to create a culture. It is a coaching book. Not a soccer coaching book.

Enjoy!

ACKNOWLEDGMENTS

I have four mentors in my life: my father, Jack Martin; my high school basketball coach, John Barker; Dr Richard Gordin, the athletics director who hired me at Ohio Wesleyan University; and Dr. Harriet Stewart, the chair of the Physical Education Department at Ohio Wesleyan University. I am lucky. These four helped me set the values and philosophy that have carried me through 46 years of coaching and teaching at Ohio Wesleyan. While much of this came from my father, all of these people were mentors. I think of them every day. Not a day goes by that I don't use something learned from them.

I would also like to acknowledge and thank my wife JoAnn Martin for putting up with me for 46 years. I don't know how she did it.

INTRODUCTION

This is not a soccer coaching book. This is a coaching book. I have been fortunate to have had some success at OWU since 1977. For specific information, please see the "About the Author" page at the end of the book. I want to share this information with you because I know we do things differently at Ohio Wesleyan. We don't talk about culture; we work culture. In many ways, culture is an overused term. Everyone talks about "culture." Many do not know what that means. Even fewer know how to create a culture. They hope it happens.

Culture does not just happen. Culture takes time and effort. Culture is a choice. You can choose to make it happen. Or you can choose not to! Many of the topics in this book you have heard of before. But I know that this book will offer another way to look at these topics. All of which are needed to develop a very positive, long-lasting culture.

We will discuss:

- The importance of a philosophy and of not having a philosophy.
- Core values and how the team should set them.
- Individual and team goal-setting strategies.
- The importance of player empowerment and leadership.
- How humility is important for all the players and teams.
- No one talks about how to prepare for adversity. We will in this book.
- What is experience? Do your players have it?
- We will introduce another level of communication.
- Great teams do the "little things."

LESSON I
THE IMPORTANCE OF A PHILOSOPHY

"Soccer players from the street are more
important than ones trained by coaches."
–Johan Cruyff

THE FOUNDATION

The foundation of my philosophy is very simple, but it makes colleagues and peers shake their heads in disbelief. **I do not believe that coaches develop players.** You simply cannot make someone else better. **Only players can make players better.** Most coaches want to believe they make players better. In fact, I know a coach that has on his business card, "*. . . the high school coach who developed (an MLS Player.)*" Sorry, coach, that is not true!

And it is the same in business; managers cannot make employees better—only employees can do that! Coaches and managers don't have this magic wand that they wave over players and employees to make them better! It is not that simple.

Every player that comes to Ohio Wesleyan must change the way he plays to make the team. This is not a negative thing. Every time a player moves "up" to a higher level, he or she must change the way they play. If a player continues to play the way he did in high school or club, he will not play at OWU. And that is the case with most college teams, at least most good college teams.

An OWU player must increase his fitness, play the ball quicker, and increase his strength. That is just a start. That is to get one foot on the practice field. To play and be successful, players must continue to get better. **But the coach cannot make the player better!** The player must do it!

Every year we have players who tell me they cannot get better. They say they are "set in their ways." The truth is, they don't want to get better because it is hard. And if they don't get better, they don't play!

The best and worst example is from the championship game in San Antonio in 2011. There were four seniors sitting on the bench next to me who did not play! Can you believe that? Senior year! National Championship game! But they did not play a minute. It was good that we won easily on Friday in the semi-final. That gave all these players a chance to see some action that weekend. But not in the final! They simply did not change the way they played from freshman to senior year.

Convincing players that the coach cannot make them better is difficult. It is hard for several reasons, but the biggest reason is our sporting culture in this country. Our system is "coach-centric." It must change to be "player centric".

American players are reactive not proactive. Players show up for practice and wait for the coach to tell them what to do. Players then react to what the coach says, and most often, players go through the motions. Players cannot get better doing this. But it is what happens in the United States. We must teach our players and employees the concept of **deliberate practice** or, as Daniel Coyle calls it in the *"Talent Code,"* **deep practice.**

THE IMPORTANCE OF PRACTICE

> *"Practice does not make perfect. Only perfect practice makes perfect."*
>
> *–Vince Lombardi*

To learn any new skill or gain expertise in a skill you need to *practice, practice, and practice some more!* No one will debate that. In fact, practice is the only place where players get better. The games are a "test" to see if the players did improve in practice. After watching a game, the coaching staff can assess where the team is in relation to the practice plans. So, the players get better in practice and **not** in the game. Which means they all must take practice seriously. After over forty years of observing top-level soccer in many countries, I can say this happens in every traditional soccer playing country. It does not happen in this country.

But it is **how** you practice that makes the difference. It is the *quality* **of your practice that is more important than the** *quantity.* Practice does not make players perfect; it makes the players' habits permanent. So, high-level practice makes high-level players. Talent does not make a big difference. Hard work and attitude make the difference.

This concept is known as *deliberate* **or** *deep practice,* **and it's incredibly powerful.**

> *"Daydreaming defeats practice; those of us who browse TV while working out will never reach the top ranks. Paying full attention seems to boost the mind's processing speed, strengthen synaptic connections, and expand or create neural networks for what we are practicing."*
>
> *–Daniel Goleman, Focus*

The common view held, until recently, was that **expert-level performance** was simply the result of **talent and "natural abilities."** This view has held back scientific progress toward learning. From a psychological perspective, what really makes experts so talented?

Experts in sport are not people with freakish natural abilities in a particular domain. Experts are experts at maintaining high levels of practice and improving performance. It's not about what you're born with. It's about how **consistently** and **deliberately** you can work to improve your performance.

So, what is deliberate or deep practice? **Deliberate/Deep practice** is a highly structured activity engaged in with the specific goal of improving performance. It requires effort, it has no monetary reward, and it is not inherently or always enjoyable. Deliberate practice takes time to improve performance, but it **will improve performance!** There are four steps to deliberate practice. When these conditions are met, practice improves accuracy and speed of performance in cognitive, perceptual, and motor tasks.

- **First, the athlete must be motivated to attend to the task and exert effort to improve performance.**
- **Second, the design of the task should consider the pre-existing knowledge of the athletes so that the task can be correctly understood after a brief period of instruction.**
- **Third, the coach should provide immediate informative feedback and knowledge of results of your performance.**
- **And finally, the athlete should repeatedly perform the same or similar tasks.**

It's important to note that, without adequate feedback about performance during practice, efficient learning is impossible, and improvement is minimal. How do you, as a coach or manager, provide feedback?

Simple practice isn't enough to rapidly gain skills. Mere repetition of an activity won't lead to improved performance. The practice must be intentional, aimed at improving performance, designed for your current skill level, and combined with immediate feedback and repetition. The player is responsible for the intentional aspect of practice. The coach is responsible for the immediate feedback!

Becoming an expert is a marathon and not a sprint. You cannot reach peak performance in just a few weeks. The practices must be deliberate and intense.

We start every practice by telling the players **what** we will do, **how** we will do it, and (most importantly) **why** we will do it. Players will be motivated if they know the why! But, in addition to that, players must come to practice with the goal of getting better. Each player must have his/her own goal for the practice session. The coaching staff have a goal for the team, but real improvement comes from players having their own goal. For example, a soccer player may go to practice with a personal goal of playing two-touch. So, for everything that happens in practice, the player plays two-touch. The player will improve technique and field vision by doing this! The player will get better. And the player will be motivated because he/she set the goal!

FEEDBACK

> *"I can't be a hypocrite as a coach because as a*
> *player that's what I wanted. I wanted feedback, I*
> *wanted communication from the boss. I showed up*
> *for work, you can yell at me if you want, but I want*
> *input. So that's the kind of coach I want to be."*
>
> *—Adam Oates, NHL Player*

In 1974, two PhD candidates in educational psychology—Ronald Gallimore and Roland Tharp—wanted to define the perfect teacher for their doctoral dissertation. They decided to use basketball coach John Wooden as the subject. Coach Wooden was very successful and still holds the record for the most NCAA Tournament Championships in basketball.

The researchers watched every practice that season and coded every comment that coach Wooden used during practice, for example, positive comment, negative comment, business comment, informational comment, etc. When asked which types of comments were used most, most respondents said, "positive comment." After all, we are told repeatedly that positive comments are very valuable for learning and self-esteem! You may be surprised to know that positive feedback was **not** the most often used. Here is a quick breakdown:

- Positive comments   about 6%
- Negative comments   about 6%
- Informational comments   about 74%

To get better, athletes need information not just positive reinforcement. A few years ago, I observed an academy session of an MLS club. The session lasted 1 hour and 15 minutes. The session focused on the near post/far post attacking part of the game. The coaches did well with a progression that moved closer and closer to game-like situations. First, the players simply delivered the ball from the wings to two teammates running into the box. Second, a third attacker was added so all three attacking positions were covered—near post, far post, and mid-goal. Third, a defender was added so the attackers could gauge the available space in the 18-yard box and attack it! Fourth, a second defender was added to make the exercise more game-like.

During the entire session the coaches did not offer one piece of information! They offered many positive comments but no information. The runs were wrong, the serves were wrong, the defenders were wrong. The exercise was a disaster. Yet the players left feeling that they got better at attacking the goals. They did not get better. They may have even gotten worse!

Doug Lemov, in his book *Practice Perfect,* offers some tips on the use of feedback in a practice setting that all coaches can use.

The coach must create an environment where feedback is used as quickly as possible and accepted. For example, in an activity where there is a line, after giving feedback, put the player back at the top of the line and not the back of the line. Have the player repeat the task immediately. Use feedback immediately! This is especially important when coaching young players.

When giving feedback, there are some immediate considerations regarding the delivery the coach must consider. Before you get pushback from a player, ask players to apply the feedback first before thinking about it. That will help the player make using feedback a habit. When the player sees improvement, the habits begin. John Wooden thought that *correction was wasted unless done immediately!* It is also important that you only give a small amount of feedback at a time. Too much information can be paralyzing.

What players do right in practice is as important as what they do wrong. *Catch them doing something right!* You want to have players repeat good behavior and understand that feedback can be both positive and negative. This will create an environment where the players understand that consistent feedback in practice makes it a normal part of the learning process. Start giving feedback immediately in the first practice; don't wait for something negative to happen!

As mentioned earlier with the example of John Wooden, information is key. Describe the solution, not the problem: Move away from using the words "don't" and "but" and tell players how they can succeed. Research suggests that one of the most demotivating aspects of sport is that coaches criticize but do not correct or provide information!

Finally, feedback does not work if the player does not understand it. Make sure that the player interprets the feedback correctly by asking the player to summarize what was said; ask players to prioritize the feedback and how they will implement feedback.

CREATE THE ENVIRONMENT

"The basic building block of good teambuilding is for a leader to promote the feeling that every human being is unique and adds value."

–Anonymous

If only players can develop players, then what is the role of the coach?

It is the coach's job to **create an environment where the player can get better (the coaching) and wants to get better (the motivation).** The environment includes the facilities, teammates, schedule, coaching, and the institution. What the player gets out of the environment is up to the player! To this end, the environment must be challenging, motivating, and fun! Players do their best work when they are having fun. Every player went to their second soccer practice because they had fun at the first practice!

With a little effort, the coaching staff can create a fun and positive environment. The players should look forward to training every day and have a smile on their face when they leave. That is not to suggest that the players shouldn't work very hard.

How can you make it fun? Competition! Everything you do in training should be competitive. Players love to play and to compete. Maybe the reds are against the grays. Every activity is competitive, and we keep score. Even an activity like a shooting "drill" is important. The team gets points for a goal and a save by their keeper. At the end of the session, there is a winner and a loser. The winning team gets their picture taken and hung up in the locker room or posted on social media. The losing team picks up the gear, does the laundry, vacuums the floor, etc. And tomorrow we will do it again!

Structuring practices so that they are competitive may be difficult at the beginning, but after a while, the coach will figure out how this works. The players will bring that competitiveness to the games. Try this great activity we learned from the late Sigi Schmid. Your players will love it.

We play "Champions League" once every week. The full team is broken down into five smaller teams. There are two fields: the champion's field and the third-place field. Games are 5–7 minutes long, and there are 7–8 games. The winner on the champion's field stays and the winner from the third-place field moves up to play the champions. The losing team on the champion's field moves down to play the fifth team, which was sitting out. The team that lost on the third-place team now must sit out.

The difference with this game is that each week the teams are different, and the scoring is individual **not** team. Each player gets three points for a win, one point for a goal, one point if the team wins by three goals or more, etc. You can add points for shutouts, points for first goal, etc. At the end of the year, there is one champion who wins a trophy!

You can add touch restrictions or any type of restriction that fits the needs of the team. This is competitive and fun. The players work extremely hard to win the cup!

So, what is our philosophy? Coaches do not make players better. Only players make players better. It is the coach's job to create an environment where the players *can* get better and *want* to get better. The environment must be motivating, competitive, and FUN!

LESSON II
TEAM AND INDIVIDUAL CORE VALUES

"Develop core team values. How do we want to
play? What are we about as a team? Who do we
want to be for one another?"
–Lindsay Gottlieb, California Golden Bears Basketball

The *forming–storming–norming–performing* model of group development was first proposed by Bruce Tuckman in 1965. Tuckman said that these phases are all necessary and inevitable in order for a team to grow, face up to challenges, tackle problems, find solutions, plan work, and deliver results. As Tuckman knew these inevitable phases were critical to team growth and development. He hypothesized that along with these factors that interpersonal relationships and \task activity would enhance the four-stage model that is needed to successfully navigate and create effective group function.

The stages are:

Forming: In the beginning, when a new team forms, individuals will be unsure of the team's purpose, how they fit in, and whether they'll work well with one another. They may be anxious, curious, or excited to get going. However, they feel, they'll be looking to the team leader for direction. This may take some time as people get to know their new colleagues and each other's ways of working. **The more the coach does in this stage to create a positive culture, the better chance the team has of getting through storming!**

Storming: In the storming stage, people start to push against the established boundaries. Conflict or friction can also arise between team members as their true characters—and their preferred ways of working—surface and clash with other people's.

At this stage, team members may challenge your authority or coaching style, or even the team's mission. Left unchecked, this can lead to face-to-face confrontations or simmering tensions.

If roles and responsibilities aren't yet clear, individuals might begin to feel overwhelmed by their workload or frustrated at a lack of progress.

Norming: Gradually, the team moves into the norming stage. People start to resolve their differences, appreciate one another's strengths, and respect your authority as a leader/coach.

Now that they know one another better, your team members will feel more comfortable asking for help and offering constructive feedback. They'll share a stronger commitment to the team's goals, and they should make good progress toward it.

Performing: Now your team is in flow and performing to its full potential. With hard work and structured processes, the team is likely to achieve its goals efficiently.

Judith Stein, from MIT's HR department, says of this stage, "Roles on the team may have become more fluid, with members taking on various roles and responsibilities as needed. Differences among members are appreciated and used to enhance the team's performance."

Most teams never get through the storming phase. You know that. How many teams have you been a part of that never reached their potential? The answer is too many. The more you do as a coach in the forming phase, the better chance you will have of getting through the storming phase.

I am not talking about "team-building" activities. You don't need those types of activities in the forming phase. The preseason is one of positive energy, hope, and the excitement of starting a new adventure.

SETTING TEAM VALUES

Core values are the foundation of what you do and why you do it. They are anchoring principles that ground you and the team to what's important and guide you and the team toward success. They are what you stand for, no matter what your circumstances may be or what your win/loss record is. Core values serve as a guide because they are non-negotiable. They serve as the essence of what your program stands for and are expected to be shared by everyone. Core values are central to your program, and the decisions leaders/coaches make should revolve around them.

Every good coach and leader understands the importance of core values as a guide through the ups and downs of sport and, more importantly, developing character in young men and women. Yet, despite the critical importance of core values, many athletic programs and teams have core values that are not clearly defined, left unstated, too flexible, and, in some cases, there are no core values at all. Sadly, too many athletic programs and teams have core values that are only an afterthought. They are not discussed and implemented, and coaches falsely assume their athletes will just pick up on these values and apply them. Without a clearly defined set of core values, many teams struggle to handle the difficulties of sport because their values change based on what's convenient in the moment rather than a stable bedrock of guiding principles. As a result, leadership is often inconsistent, there is little accountability between teammates, and the potential to build character through sport is lost.

As a coach and leader, developing and communicating core values begins and ends with you, the coach. However, because core values are central to team success and character development, it is vital to involve your team in determining them, making them visible, emphasizing them, and using them as a guide for your program's daily decisions and actions.

To begin defining your program's core values, consider the following categories of core values. Have a meeting with your team and staff. Ask yourself and your team, what do we value most? It is very important that the team develops the core values. **This ensures "buy in" as the season progresses.**

Ask yourself and the team, what do we value most?

- Being people of strong character.
- Effort and commitment.
- Having a positive and productive attitude.
- Being a good teammate.
- Competing relentlessly.

I will now share the process used at Ohio Wesleyan, which begins on the first day of preseason. Each senior has a group of underclassmen and a list of values. The groups find a spot at the facility to list their top 10 values. The whole team reconvenes, and the captains collate the values on the white board until the list is between 10 to 12 values. This is a guide. Your list may vary. **This is run totally by the seniors and the players. The coaching staff have nothing to do with this process! This is very important. The players are more likely to "buy in" if they create the values!**

The groups go back to their spot and come back with the top five values. The seniors lead what is usually a spirited discussion to get down to our 7 to 10 values for the year.

There are three general types of values:

Stay: Most of the group agrees the value is important and will be a core value. Example: "RESPONSIBILITY: We will be responsible for our actions. No excuses!"

Combine:	Two or more values that are similar can be merged into one overarching value. Example: Poise and maturity can be combined into "COMPOSURE: We will control our emotions and decisions on and off the field."
Cut:	Most of the team agrees that the idea does not have enough relevance or support to be a core value.

Once your team has developed 7 to 10 core values, it's time to put them into action. Here are a few ways to make your team's core values part of its daily commitment to progress and success.

1. POST YOUR CORE VALUES IN YOUR LOCKER ROOM

Create a constant reminder of your core values by posting them in the locker room, weight room, and your coaches' offices. This doesn't have to be anything fancy, only consistently visible. Here is an example from the OWU values program:

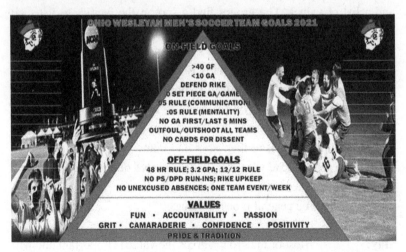

2. HAVE EVERY MEMBER OF YOUR TEAM AND STAFF MEMORIZE YOUR CORE VALUES

To help embed core values, have your team members and staff memorize the core values. Be sure everyone in the program can recite the core values at a moment's notice. We have every member of the team sign the poster above. It is hung in a strategic place in the locker room. Do the players read it every day? Of course not. But it is there. There is a subtle imprint that takes place each day.

3. EMPHASIZE ONE OF YOUR CORE VALUES EACH WEEK

Make a full week all about one of your core values. Before the first practice of the week, discuss the core value that will be emphasized that week and why it's important. After each practice that week, recognize those that committed to and best exhibited that core value.

4. RECOGNIZE YOUR CORE VALUES WHEN YOU SEE THEM ON AND OFF THE FIELD

Call out your team members and staff when they exemplify the team's core values. Catch them "doing good" and use them as an example for the entire team. Don't be afraid to stop practice for a minute to point out how hard someone is working or when someone is being a great teammate.

5. INCORPORATE YOUR CORE VALUES IN YOUR HIGHLIGHT VIDEOS

Be sure to include core values in your highlight and video sessions. This is a great way to show what your core values look like and to recognize those committed to them. It's also a great way to show why core values are important, even if the result of a play or a game isn't what you want. These highlights are about doing it right.

It will be easy to stick to your core values when everything is going well. It's easy to preach core values when your team is winning, everyone is healthy, and team chemistry is good. Sticking to core values becomes more difficult when you're on a losing streak, you're faced with setbacks, and your athletes may not be doing the right things on and off the field. As previously mentioned, core values begin and end with you, the coach. When you bend and break your core values, you run the risk of losing respect and trust with your team, and you send the message that shortcuts are okay. Stick to your core values. They are an invaluable resource to build mentally tough athletes and develop character in those around you.

As an example, the OWU team of 2022 had the worst start in the program's history. We were 0-4-2. What did we do? Nothing different. We stuck to our values. We didn't give up a goal in October; won the conference championship; made the NCAA Tournament; and ended up with an 11-5-3 record. Values work!

INDIVIDUAL VALUES

Once team values are complete, it might be useful to have each team member create their own Values List. Many of the team members will have values. Few will have written them down. As you know, when you write something down, you own it.

VALUES ASSIGNMENT

This exercise is designed to help you reach a better understanding of your most important values.

STEP 1: WHAT I VALUE MOST
Read the documents that offer sample values to get an understanding of what values are and to understand that there are many values.

Select your **10 most significant values.**

STEP 2: ELIMINATION

Now that you have identified the initial 10, imagine that you are only allowed five values. List your top five values. Explain in a sentence or two why you chose each value.

Now imagine you can only have four values. What are they? Why?

Now you can only have three values. What are they? Why?

Now you have only two values. What are they? Why?

What is your most important value? Why

As mentioned previously, the more you do in the forming phase, the better the chance of getting through storming. This process is totally run by the players. You—as the coach—and team leaders can refer to these values as the season moves on. These values are the fundamental guide to all team, player, and coach behavior!

LESSON III
TEAM AND INDIVIDUAL GOALS

"All successful people have a goal. No one can get anywhere unless he/she knows where he/she wants to go and what he/she wants to be or do."
–Norman Vincent Peale, an OWU graduate

In 1977, I had finished almost all my requirements for the PhD at Ohio State. I needed only two credits to graduate. I found a course in the Ohio State Business School entitled MBO: Management by Objectives. At that time, MBO was a new concept in management theory. Management theory was changing from the "my-way-or-the-highway" approach to a more "humanistic" approach. The emphasis of MBO was one-on-one management and not "mass management." The emphasis and focus began to move from the "boss/coach-centric" approach to the "subordinate/player-centric" approach.

MBO is basically a one-on-one approach that used goal setting as motivation. The key was that the subordinate (player) set the goals for him/herself, not the boss (coach). As the semester ran to completion, I could not help but feel this was something I could use as a coach. The same dynamic was starting to happen in coaching. That is, we were beginning to move from a coach-centric my-way-or-the-highway approach to a player-centric approach.

From the first day I set foot on the OWU campus, all the teams I coached used MBO. I changed the acronym to mean *Motivation by Objectives*. This led to the goal-setting process I have used—with tweaks—for over 46 years.

Did it work? Yes, the goal setting we have used for the past 46 years has worked very well. Here are a few examples:

- I cannot count the number of times that alums have referred to our goal-setting process with the words, "I still use goal setting in my business today."
- The win-loss record in the two sports I coached (soccer and lacrosse) is 854-172-79. The winning percentage is 83%. And MBO is the only common denominator for both teams.
- I have many examples of how MBO has worked over the years. Let me share one example so you get the idea. A few years ago, a junior forward came to me in preseason with his goal-setting sheet. He had three goals:
  - » To score a goal in each game.
  - » To break all the OWU scoring records.
  - » To be an All-America.

We met to go over the goals and create a plan. His evaluation suggested that he was a great athlete. He was great in the air and had a tremendous left foot. But he could hardly stand on his right foot. It was clear that for him to reach his goals, he would have to improve his right foot. We made a plan.

He came out with me before every practice and helped warm up the keepers using only his right foot. This was a low-pressure, high-repetition activity. Like many coaches, we end each training session with a game. The player and I agreed when he played in the end game, any time he used his left foot would be a turnover. This was high pressure, low repetition.

I wouldn't be using this example if he didn't reach all three goals. He was a two-time All-American. He averaged 1.29 goals/game his last two years. He still holds the OWU scoring record. And in his senior season, he scored one more goal with his right foot than his left foot! MBO works.

Goal setting is the number one strategy to develop and enhance intrinsic motivation. The OWU soccer program is all about intrinsic motivation. Here is what the MBO cycle at OWU looks like:

Motivation by Objectives

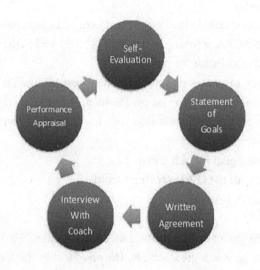

WHY MBO?

MBO provides the coach, player, and team with many advantages:

- It is the main strategy to develop **intrinsic motivation.**
- A rousing pre-game speech does not work when teams play a lot of games.
- It creates motivation without emotion. The number one cause for loss of skill is fatigue. The second cause is uncontrolled emotions.
- The goals are created by the player, not the coach. The player owns his/her goals.
- Goal setting is challenging for the players.
- MBO increases player self-esteem.
- The result is easy to measure.

WHAT IS A GOAL?

Goal setting is both an art and a science. The first (or even second) time the players try setting goals, the goals won't be any good. But the more the players set goals, the better the goals will become. And the more intrinsic motivation will improve.

As you present goal setting to your team, it is important the team members know what a goal is:

- A goal is the object or the aim and direction of the players efforts.
- Goals satisfy a need i.e., the need for achievement = All-America as a goal.
- Numbers goals are used to increase production i.e., *I will score a goal each game.*
- A behavioral goal changes behavior i.e., *to be an All-America I have to improve my fitness, my shot, my attitude. etc.*
- The best goals are a combination of numbers and behaviors i.e., *to score one goal a game I need to improve my fitness, work on my weak foot, come early to practice and stay late.*

Once the players understand what a goal is, they can begin the process. That means the players should understand what makes a goal meaningful. You have all heard about SMART goals. Before goals can be created, the players must have a clear understanding of SMART goals.

A goal must be:

Specific: *I want to score one goal a game.* That is very specific. Many players will say, *I want to be a better soccer player.* Although we all understand what this means, it is not specific enough!

Measurable: The goal of scoring one goal each game is very specific and very measurable. The goal of becoming a better soccer player is just not measurable!

Achievable:	The player must be able to reach the stated goal. This is where consultation with the coach becomes important. If the player sets a goal of being an All-American, it must be achievable. The coach may have to suggest that, at this point, the player will not be able to achieve All-American status. The coach will then help the player find a goal that might be challenging but more achievable. Goal setting is all about intrinsic motivation. If the goal is too difficult (being an All-American), it will build frustration in the player and impact motivation negatively. If the goal is too easy (I want to make the team), it is demotivating. What happens when you make the team?
Relevant:	The goal must be relevant to the situation. In this case, the goals should be soccer-oriented specifically and about the current season.
Time Sensitive:	The player must set a time stamp. Usually, the time stamp is the length of the season. The time stamp is used to motivate the player. For example, *I want to lose 10 pounds. I want to lose 10 pounds by October 1st.* The time stamp acts as a motivator and prevents procrastination.

The OWU Motivation by Objectives serves many purposes for our team achievement and team culture. It is used to set both players' goals and team goals. For the players, MBO will:

- **Help the players with practice preparation:** We expect each player to have a goal or two for each practice. The coaching staff has a goal for each session. But to improve, the players must have a goal or two for practice. For example, the player's goal might be to improve field vision. The plan for the player in practice might be to play only two-touch. That way the player is getting better at something he/she needs to work on in the context of the team training session.

- **Help the players focus on improving:** Instead of the player setting a goal "to get better," or "be a better player," MBO helps the player be very specific about what and how they should get better. For example, the goal is to make All Conference. The plan is to increase fitness, work on field vision, etc.
- **Help fix a player "slump":** Sometimes goal setting can become a burden. Instead of using MBO to improve in the context of the game, the player might focus only on the goal(s). The coach and player can meet during the season and "reset" goals to help the player out of a slump. A few years ago, we had a forward who was elected captain. He set a goal of scoring 20 goals in the season. He pressed too much and was really struggling. He had scored only three goals by the halfway point of the season. The coaching staff met with the player and helped him reset his goals. We dropped the number of goals he would score from 20 to 11. He broke out of the slump and finished strong and ended up scoring 13 goals.

Goal setting also helps the team. The first day of preseason, the players set team goals (more on this later). The coaching staff is not involved at all. This helps the players "buy in" to the entire goal-setting process. The end product comes from the team, not the coach! This is important. Goal setting will:

- **Help the players focus as the season goes on:** When the dog days of the season hit, the coach can remind the players that their goals are not being achieved. It serves as a reboot and increased focus.
- **Team slump:** There will be a time during the season when the team will not be performing up to its potential. Once again, the coach can remind the team of **their** goals (i.e., winning the conference) to get the team back on track.
- **Practice motivation:** Before practice for a big game, the coach can remind the team of their goals to improve concentration in practice. For example, *tomorrow we play a conference opponent. One of the goals you set was to win the conference. So, let's have a good practice today so we can do well tomorrow!*

What is the OWU Motivation by Objectives (MBO)?

- **MBO is a one-on-one process.** The coach and the player work together to create the goals.
- **The standard:** Setting a standard is very important. The coach must evaluate the team and players realistically. Then the coach must set realistic standards against which individual performance is measured. These standards should not reflect what the players (and team) feel they ought to do, rather what you—the coach—expects them to do!
- **The evaluation:** The player and coach each evaluate the player. The player will not get better if he/she does not know where they really are as a soccer player. This is very hard. Most players don't do well at first with a self-evaluation.
- **Statement of goals:** After the self-evaluation, the player sets goals based on the strengths and weaknesses as discovered in the evaluation.
- **Written agreement between the player and the coach:** At this point, the coach can help refine the goals and make sure they are reachable for the player. The player and coach then write the goals down and both sign the document.
- **Develop a plan of action:** If there is no plan, there are no goals. The player will not wake up one day as an All-American. There must be a plan to get there.
- **Performance appraisal:** The coach and player monitor the player's progress to ascertain if the player is on the right track. If not, adjustments can be made to the goal(s).
- **Appraisal interview:** After the season, the coach and player meet. Were the goals achieved? If so, why? If not, why not?
- **Start again!**

THE OHIO WESLEYAN UNIVERSITY GOAL SETTING CASE STUDY

We set team goals first. In Lesson II we discussed how we set the team's core values. The exercise is totally led by the team leaders. Not the coaching staff. After we have our core values, we set the team goals. The procedure is the same as we use to set the values.

Each senior gets a group of underclassmen. Each group finds a spot in the facility/locker room for their group. The leaders are given 20 minutes to come up with their on-field goals first. The whole team reconvenes in the locker room. The captains collate all the on-field goals first. The list is reduced to the top 10 or 12 goals. The groups go back to their spots and come back with five goals. From those goals, the team identifies 8 to 10 team on-field goals. The goals will include how many goals we want to score, how many goals we will allow, how we will perform at home, how we will perform on the road, etc. The same procedure is followed for off-field goals that will include GPA, alcohol/drug use, etc. See diagram for the finished product.

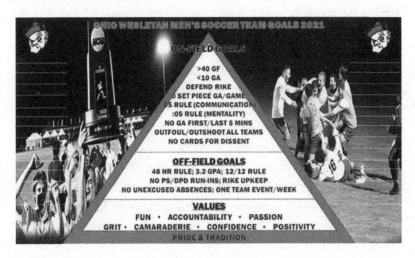

PLAYER GOAL SETTING

Step one begins in preseason, and we begin the process of goal setting for individual players. It is important that the players understand the standards of the program and an understanding of how we want to play the game. Research is very clear. The more the players understand expectations, the better chance they have of playing at a high level. We give the team and player standards using the document, Jay Martin's *Definition of Good Soccer*. This instrument can be found in Appendix A.

Step two is the self-evaluation. The evaluation instrument can be found in Appendices B and C. On the first page we evaluate fitness, mental toughness, and technique. The second page is position specific. We evaluate what the player does when we have the ball and what he does while defending. Both the player and the coaching staff evaluate the player. This is important to clarify the strengths and weaknesses of the player. When the players first do this, they usually do one of two things. They evaluate themselves very positively or they beat themselves up. Having the coaching staff evaluate the players will add a bit of realism to the process. By the time the player is a junior, there is no longer a need for the coaching staff to evaluate the player. By that time the players understand the process. The player and the coach sit down and go over the evaluation together. There is a discussion of the differences in the evaluation. The player and the coach come to an agreement on the strengths and weaknesses of the player.

Step three is the review session. After the self-evaluation, the players complete the MBO sheet. This is in Appendix D. Then the player and coach are ready for the review session. This is a very important meeting. The review session is a one-on-one meeting between the coach and the player. The meeting sets the tone for the player for the upcoming season. Using the MBO document, the player sets goals for the season. After the goals are set, the player and coach meet. In this review session the coach and player will:

- Review the goals to ensure they are SMART goals. This is very important for all new players. Most players will not have SMART goals when they start the goal-setting process. The goals will look like *I want to be a better soccer player*. That is not good enough. This is the time to modify the goals if necessary.
- Discuss the players' strengths and weaknesses. There must be some agreement between the coach and player regarding the evaluation. **Players will not get better unless they know accurately and honestly where they are as a player.**
- Discuss the changes the player must make to reach the goals. These changes may include increased fitness, improving technique, etc.
- Discuss the potential obstacles. Goal setting is used to increase motivation. If a player does not reach a goal, there may be a reason. Knowing the reason may help the player understand why he/she missed the goal. For example, if a player has a goal of being an All-America, he/she must understand that selection is a process of a committee and not solely due to how well the player played!
- Discuss and create a plan of action. Without a plan there are no goals! The plan should be written and agreed upon by the coach and player. We use the MBO instrument in the appendix.

Remember that the purpose of goal setting is to increase motivation. If goals are too high or too low, motivation is lost!

Step four is the appraisal interview. This is the second one-on-one meeting between the coach and player. This should take place at a predetermined time. At OWU we meet during the fourth week of the season. If changes need to be made, this timetable allows the player to make changes and redefine goals. The agenda for this meeting looks like this:

- Review goals and agree on changes. As previously mentioned, if the player set a goal of scoring 20 goals and they only have four at this meeting, the goal should be revised.

- Discuss and recognize the progress and achievement being made.
- Discuss and let the player know where he/she stands in the team.
- Discuss and identify potential if the changes are made.
- Encourage self-development. Only players can make themselves better. The sooner a player understands that, the sooner the player has a chance to get better. If the player continues to wait for the coach to make him/her better, they will never improve!
- Record the results of the meeting. I keep the results of every meeting for the players for 4 years. This helps the player with the goal-setting process going forward.

Step five is simply . . . start over!

As the process continues through the players' four years on campus, goal setting will:

- Help increase work rate and quality of work.
- Help make work more meaningful.
- Help clarify the coach's expectations of the players and team.
- Help share the responsibility from player and coach.
- Help keep internal competition at a healthy level.
- Help improve intrinsic motivation!

There are, of course, potential problems that may arise during the process. The coach must be aware of these problems to make the process run smoothly. These problems include:

- Pushing too hard. A "big" goal leads to a big risk and may cause big failure!
- The goal becomes a ceiling. I want to make the team! What happens when the player makes the team? What's next?
- Ignoring areas where goals are not set. Players may focus on goals so much (for example, *improving my weak foot*) that they forget to work on overall technique or other aspects of their game.

- Using goals as a tool for punishment. Players should not be punished if they don't achieve a goal. This type of action will undermine a positive environment.
- Dishonesty. Players may be dishonest about reaching goals.
- Failure by the coach to explain how individual goals mesh with team goals. A player who wants to score a goal in each game must do so in the context of the team tactics. The player should not shoot every time he/she gets the ball!

A WORD ABOUT IMPROVING

Goal setting helps athletes improve. That is what we, as coaches, try to do every day. It is important to understand that. But, I believe, Americans spend too much time working on weaknesses at the expense of working on their strengths. Look at three columns. The left column is for weaknesses. The middle column is for manageable skills—not strengths and not weaknesses, but skills that are useful and usable for the player. The column on the right is for strengths. I don't think it is possible to move a weakness from the first column to the third column. We can move it to the manageable column, but not the strengths column. We should understand our strengths and play to our strengths. That's what great players do. Franz Beckenbauer had a strong right foot. He used that foot much more than his left!

GAME GOALS

After the practice the day before each game, we give the players the Game Goal sheet (see Appendix E). The sheet has three columns for the players to complete and one for the coaching staff after the game.

Column one:	Goals for the game
Column two:	Potential obstacles
Column three:	Personal action plan

The same rules apply to the game goals as the season goals. The players use the SMART acronym to prepare for the game. Column four is a post-game evaluation by the coaching staff. Here is an example:

GAME GOALS FOR A CENTER BACK

Goal: No shots for the opposing striker
Potential obstacle: The striker is an All-American and conference-leading scorer
Action plan: Don't let him get the ball
                         If he gets the ball, don't let him turn
                         If he turns, force him wide
                         Block the shot or pass (no tackle)

We want the players going on the field and thinking about their action goals rather than winning. This promotes focus on the process and not the outcome. That is the foundation of our program!

LESSON IV
PLAYER LEADERSHIP

---

*"Leaders become great not because of
their power, but because of their ability to
empower others."*
–John Maxwell

This is a player-owned program. The players are here for four years, and, in that time, it is their program. They help make all major decisions. The players' input is important to the success of the team/program. A good program is different from a good team. A team meets every day to practice for 2 hours. A program encompasses the other 22 hours. We have a good program, and it is player owned.

By creating a positive environment, the coach creates an emotional bond between the players and the program. The program becomes more meaningful for the players than just belonging to a team. The players have a vested interest that goes beyond what happens on the field. This bond motivates the players every day. They **want** to do what is best for the team/program. We want the players to look forward to training every day and have a smile on their face when they leave. With a little creativity and thought the coach can make the training session positive, competitive, efficient, and fun!

The bond is carried with the players long after graduation. The bond and the relationships made in the program complement the academic mission of the institution. Something special happens in this program. There is a connection between the players on the team, between the players from all generations, and between the players and the University!

EMPOWERMENT

A good coach prepares everyone in the program to leave starting the first day they join the program, regardless of whether they are players or assistant coaches. For this to happen, players must learn valuable lessons about themselves and about working with others. Players cannot learn these lessons in a coach-centered team. A coach-centered team is "old school" and it is simply a "my-way-or-the-highway" environment. A coach-centered team revolves around the coach telling the players (and assistant coaches) what to do and how to do it. Very seldom does a coach in this environment explain *why* we are doing it. Explaining the *why* is motivating for the players: here is *what* we are going to do, and therefore we are going to do it!

Coaches are control freaks. Most believe that to be successful they must control everything about an athlete and the team. Many of the old-school coaches look down on the player-centered coach because they, the player-centered coach, allow players to do what they want and thinks that the player-centered coach acts as if he/she is the best friend of the player(s). The old-school coaches believe a coach should be an authority figure. The old schoolers believe that player-centered coaches are soft, weak-minded, and allow players to disrespect them. That perception is simply not true!

Dr. Lynn Kidman is a senior lecturer at Auckland University in New Zealand has long been a proponent of player-centered coaching. In her 2001 book, *Developing Decision Makers,* she offers this as a definition of player-centered coaching and the reason(s) this is so important:

> "Player centered coaching emphasizes giving players autonomy for decision making with the clear intention of empowering athletes to make choices, develop higher levels of motivation (individually and as a team) and learn how to develop solutions designed to enhance their performance."

Dr. Kidman's research suggests that player-centered coaching can lead to increased player engagement, better communication between players and the coach, improved competence, and a higher level of motivation to perform.

Empowerment works! Earlier we discussed how to get players to "buy-in." We discussed value and goal setting as ways to start the process of buy-in. Empowering players is the ultimate and final step to get the players to buy-in. Empowerment creates an emotional attachment to the program by the players. The team means more to each player than an activity that takes place between 4 p.m. and 6 p.m.!

Soccer is not like other sports. Soccer is a player-driven sport. Soccer is about players making decisions quickly. Players must learn to make these decisions without relying on the coach. The coach can tell the players what the solution is, or the coach can create a series of questions that guide the player to solve the problem.

Dr. Kidman suggests that small-sided games and subsequent questioning of the players will move the individual and the team toward empowerment. Players are more motivated to play a game than to engage in a drill. Every soccer coach has used a "keep away" type game to teach the importance of possession. Most coaches will ask the team with the ball to make a certain number of passes. The good coach will add restrictions to the game to make success easier or harder to achieve.

For example, there are two teams in a 20 by 20-yard grid. The object of the game is for one team to make 10 consecutive passes without turning the ball over. This game challenges the players to devise solutions to be successful and make 10 passes in a row. When the team loses the ball, the coach should not **tell** the players why they lost the ball. Rather, the coach should empower the players to become more involved in their own improvement, decision making, and problem solving by asking questions:

- How did your body position affect your ability to keep the ball?
- How could you improve the passing angle?

- What do you have to do to solve this problem successfully and make 10 passes in a row?
- What worked? What did not work? What will you do differently next time?

We are concerned about our players' overall development as young people moving toward adulthood. They must learn to perform and make their own decisions in practice and competition. This simply means they must be allowed to make mistakes! In fact, mistakes should be encouraged. A positive coaching environment relies on the players making mistakes and learning from them. We allow that to happen. We want that to happen.

Soccer is a negative game. More things go wrong than go right. That is why, on average, only two or three goals are scored in soccer. Can you imagine an NBA game played for 90 minutes instead of the 48 minutes played now? What would the scores be? I think about 270-260! Basketball is more controllable. Soccer is not.

We never yell at players for making a mistake. We never yank a player out of the game for making a mistake. We never punish a player in practice the next day for making a mistake. Real coaching empowers the players to identify the mistake, learn from the mistake, and become a better player because of the process.

Humor is important. As mentioned, soccer is a negative game. The coach (and other players) must not pile on a mistake. That increases the negative environment. Rather we should laugh. The coach-centered coach would not like this. Laughter would be considered an insult to the coach and the game. An example from the highest level:

A few years ago, I visited FC Bayern Munich for three weeks to observe the club and the training techniques. One day I was observing the second team. Thomas Müller was performing a shooting drill. Müller is now on Bayern's first team and a member of the 2014 World Cup winning

German team. The exercise began with the player on the 6-yard line facing the goal. There is a player at each goal post with soccer balls. On the signal, Müller backpedaled to the top of the 18-yard box. The players on the post hit hard low passes to Müller who tried to shoot the ball into the goal. Each session was 90 seconds. This is quite difficult. The shooter must change his balance, stop the backward momentum, and strike the ball cleanly. Müller, one of today's best players in the world, did not make one shot. He hit the ball over the goal, off the cross bar, off the post. What did he do? He fell to the ground laughing hysterically! No pressure. Nothing negative. Simply a great understanding of how difficult soccer is and humor.

WE LEADERSHIP

"The ratio of We's to I's is the best indicator of the development of a team."

–Lewis B. Ergen

As part of the environment, there must be standards and expectations. One of the standards we set is that the OWU men's soccer team is a **WE** and **US** organization not an **I** or **ME** organization. Although there are few rules on the team, one hard and fast rule is not using the words **I** or **ME**. We don't want the players talking about **themselves** in high school or club soccer; we want the players focusing on **US.**

In 2012, 14 business, government, and educational leaders in Central Ohio created the Ross Leadership Foundation (RLI). The prime mover with this Foundation was Dr. Paul Otte, formerly the president of Franklin University in Columbus. I am one of the founders of the RLI. The entire Foundation is based on **WE** leadership.

THE LEADERSHIP COUNCIL

In a coach-centered team, the coach is responsible for everything that happens in the program and the players are accountable to the coach. That is not how the OWU program works.

We have a Leadership Council (LC) that holds players accountable and is responsible for the team. The LC was the idea of one of our former players, and we have used a council for many years. The LC is comprised of the captains and an elected representative from each class. The LC performs a variety of duties:

- The LC acts as a conduit between team members and the coaching staff.
- The LC helps decide who we will play each year.
- The LC selects the uniforms and gear we will use.
- The LC makes sure that all team "chores" are taken care of by the players.
- The LC is responsible for any punishment necessary for an infraction of any rules.

The LC and coaches meet every Monday. At that time, we review where we are in the season and look ahead to the games this week. The players are encouraged to voice any concerns they and/or the players they represent might have. Is the team tired? How is training going? Is anyone causing problems on the team? How is the morale? What are our priorities for this week? Many times, there are lively discussions and even disagreements on a point or situation. But when we walk out the door, we are all on the same page.

The question of punishment or consequences is always a difficult one on any team. If the star quarterback does something stupid and gets in trouble, should he be suspended? If he is suspended, the entire team is penalized, not just the quarterback. So, what is a fair way to punish players without punishing the team? A few years ago, the LC offered a solution. They came up with a list of problems and a punishment for each. The punishment was defined by community service hours for the offender. The idea was that the player who made the mistake is punished and not the whole team. Community service hours could include:

- Doing the post-game or practice laundry
- Picking up trash
- Emptying trash cans
- Vacuuming the locker room floor
- Picking up the gear after training
- Sweeping the bleachers

The number of community service hours is dictated by the severity of the problem. For example:

- Failure to complete a "chore"   3 hours
- Late to training/meeting   3 hours
- No hustle in training   4 hours
- Open container (of beer) on campus   6 hours
- Underage drinking   8 hours

You get the picture. As with all proposals, the team voted on this. It passed and is now in use every year. Here is an example of the LC at work.

> A few years ago, one of our players was arrested for having marijuana and smoking paraphernalia in his room. It was clear that he was not only using but also selling marijuana. The local courts put him on probation. The LC felt that they had to address this situation. They did not have community service hours for this type of offense. So, the council met and decided on the following:

- He would be suspended for eight games but had to attend every team function—including practice. He was not a starter or even a very good player, but the LC felt that ". . . he needed the team more than the team needed him.
- He had to have a weekly meeting with a drug and alcohol counselor and provided a written note to the coach each week.
- He had to visit every elementary school in the town and tell students why they should not use alcohol or marijuana. He had to schedule these meetings with the principal and was accompanied by a member of the LC!
- He did the team laundry for the duration of the eight games. That was about five weeks.

What a great educational experience this was for the team, the members of the LC, and for the offender! And if everything on a college campus should be educational, this fits!

LESSON V
HUMILITY

---

*"There is nothing noble in being superior to
your fellow man; true nobility is being superior
to your former self."*
–Ernest Hemingway

*"I believe the first test of a truly great man is in
his humility."*
–John Ruskin

Humility is a very important and necessary part being of a good team and a good player. But it is very difficult to teach. This is very true today because, in our athletic culture, good athletes are put on a pedestal early and often. So, players coming into college are often not very humble and not very interested in being humble.

But it is not their fault. It is the fault of our sporting culture. How often is a very good high school athlete walking down the hall in his high school and hears, *"Hey Joe, great goal last night!"* You never hear, *"Hey Joe, great math test yesterday!"* Never! The athlete is programmed for sports to mean more than academics. So, the athlete comes to college feeling that success in sports is due to his or her talent and ability. Hard work has nothing to do with it!

In addition, college-aged students are in a very important time in life that lends itself to a high level of conceit. Up to the freshman year, most students have been dependent upon their parents and family. The parents made many, if not all, of the important decisions. Now in their first year, the students seek and crave total independence. Now there is a coach telling them that they have to give in to a team. Giving in (again) is not high on the students' list. They do not understand that interdependence is the best place to be! And to get there, they need to develop humility!

There is no improvement as a player or as a team without humility. This is true because the first step leading to humility is an honest self-evaluation. The key word is honest, and you can't be honest without being humble. If you think you have made it and you are as good as you can be, you will not get better. In fact, you won't even try to get better because you are already great!

SELF-EVALUATION

We start the self-evaluation process during preseason of the freshman year. We mentioned the self-evaluation briefly in Lesson II. Self-evaluation is important in the goal-setting exercise that the player undertakes each year. We have an instrument that we use for the players; the self-evaluation form is in Appendix B.

The first page of the instrument is the same for every player (except goalkeepers) and is broken into three parts that reflect three of the four pillars of soccer:

- **The Mental:** The areas include coachability, commitment, desire to improve, leadership, focus, maturity, etc.
- **The Physical:** This section evaluates quickness, speed, strength, endurance, etc.
- **The Technical:** This section deals with certain technical skills that all players must have to play.

The second page is position-specific and deals with the specific attacking and defending roles for the position. The scale is 1–5, with one being excellent and 5 being really bad. It is not unusual for freshmen to rank themselves very high the first two or three times they evaluate themselves. That changes over time!

As mentioned, the player evaluates himself and the coaching staff evaluates the player. Humility begins to take hold. The player begins to understand that he is not perfect and that he is not the best. At this point, the player begins the process of developing. A good, hard, and honest assessment is the first step!

As mentioned in Lesson II, this step is the first step for individual goal setting and the first step toward gaining an understanding of humility.

TEAM HUMILITY

We do many things each year that help the team understand the essence of humility. We want the players to understand that they are not better than anyone else. As a result, we have the following as part of the program:

Facility Maintenance: We do not allow the university crew to do anything at our facility except cut and line the field. We take care of "our" house. We clean the locker room, the restrooms, the bleachers, we empty the trash and do all the day-to-day maintenance necessary.

Laundry: We do all our own laundry—both practice gear and game uniforms.

Clinics: We offer free soccer clinics for the county. In addition, when we go to Germany (every three years) we stay in a small town called Baumholder. Baumholder is home to one of the largest US Army bases outside the United States. The first day on the ground, we offer a free soccer clinic for the children of the soldiers who are serving in the Middle East!

Spring Cleaning: We help some of the spring sports prepare their field(s) for the upcoming season. We weed the skin of the baseball and softball fields, put in sod, trim shrubs, etc.

Special Olympics: We are active in the Special Olympic movement in Central Ohio.

Humility is very important and leads to "giving back" as the players move through their lives!

LESSON VI
ADVERSITY

*"One thing about championship teams is that
they're resilient. No matter what is thrown at
them, no matter how deep the hole, they find a way
to bounce back and overcome adversity."*
–Nick Saban, Alabama football

One of the things that has always bothered me about coaches is the way they treat adversity. Every coach I know talks about dealing with adversity. They suggest that participation in sport will prepare the athlete to handle adversity. But very few coaches tell their team **how** to deal with adversity. I do believe that participation in sport **can** prepare you to deal with adversity. But does that always happen? I do not think so.

At OWU we teach our athletes what adversity is and how to deal with it! The first step in dealing with adversity is the culture we have created. The culture starts day one in preseason when the team sets the core values for the season and the goals for the season. This is done entirely by the senior players. They lead the rest of the team through the process. Having a strong value and team goal culture prepares the players to accept and deal with adversity. Here is the finished product from the 2011 team. It is the team that won a national championship and had to deal with adversity on the way.

In addition to the core values and team goals, we prepare the team to face situations in several ways. Each season, the seniors are given a book to read and present to the team on days when we have inclement weather. I know that players don't like to practice in bad weather. There is very little learning that happens on those days. We rotate books each year so that after 4 years, the players are introduced to many different books.

Although the list changes each year, the following is a partial list of books we have used in the past.

Team Building—Michels
Success is a Choice—Pitano
Talent Code—Coyle
Leading with the Heart—Coach K
The 7 Habits of Highly Effective People—Covey
Sacred Hoops—Jackson
Leading at the Edge—Shackelton
Thinking Fast and Slow—Kahneman
The Winner Within—Riley
The Team Captain's Leadership Manual—Janssen
On Becoming a Leader—Bennis
The Culture Code—Coyle
Outliers—Gladwell
Mindset—Dweck
Grit—Duckworth

The Art of Learning—Waitzkin
Talent is Overrated—Colvin
Game Changer—Connelly
The Leadership Lessons of Greg Popovich—Popovich
The Score Takes Care of Itself—Walsh
Win Forever—Carroll
Leading—Ferguson

In 2011, one of these books was *Bounce* by Keith McFarland. The book was written for businesses. But there are similarities between an athletics team and a business. The book was about a man who was losing his company because of some unforeseen problems—that is adversity. While at a gym, he met a former Green Beret. A friendship developed. The Green Beret shared the lessons he learned in boot camp about dealing with adversity. The lessons were learned and followed, and the company was saved. Although we rotate the books, we read this book each year so the players are introduced to dealing with adversity.

The steps McFarland recommends for dealing with adversity in his book *Bounce* are:

1. Embrace the Bounce
2. Manage the Anxiety
3. Manage the Mental Factors
4. Manage the Money
5. Manage the Mission
6. Manage the Morale

As mentioned earlier, the book was written for businesses. All the examples in the book are related to the story and the business "bouncing back" from adversity. These steps can also be used to deal with athletic anxiety and adversity.

The first week of December in 2011, the OWU soccer team flew to San Antonio, Texas, to compete in the NCAA Division III soccer championship. Upon arrival, we rented three vans and two cars. The original plan was to check into the hotel, change and go to Trinity University for a training session.

On the way to the hotel, we stopped for lunch. While eating lunch, two of our vans were vandalized. Everything in each van was stolen. We lost 15 computers and all the uniforms and clothes for each player in the vans. The players had absolutely nothing. This was real adversity. We immediately began using the steps from *Bounce* to deal with the problem.

Embrace the Bounce: The first step in dealing with adversity is recognizing there is a problem. Many people in these types of situations try to push the problem away or don't accept the reality. We immediately called the team together in the parking lot and explained that this really happened. We, as a group, had to accept that. We had to embrace adversity. We had to change the mindset from a "feeling-sorry-for-ourselves" thought process to an "okay-this-happened-let's-move-forward" thought process. We understood that this was easier said than done, but we had to get the players thinking forward.

Manage the Anxiety: This was the week before final examinations at OWU. Losing the computers was a real problem. Most of the players had final projects, papers, and study material on their computers. "What am I going to do?" was a common question we had to deal with to move forward. We felt if we could ease the academic anxiety, it would help the players regain focus on the national championship. We immediately called the university president and told him what happened. Within an hour every faculty member knew what happened and who was involved. The president asked the faculty to be supportive and sympathetic of the situation and with these students in the next week. The faculty agreed. Many of the players were economic students. There was a huge accounting final on Tuesday of the following week. Two accounting professors flew to San Antonio at their own expense to help the students prepare. They met with the students individually and in groups and reviewed the material in preparation for the exam. The academic anxiety decreased immediately.

Manage the Mental Factors: With the academic pressure reduced a bit, we turned to manage the mental side of things. We changed all our plans. We did not want the players to go back to the hotel, sit in their room, and worry about the situation. We wanted them to be active, to get their minds on something else. We decided to go to Trinity and train immediately. Paul McGinlay, the Trinity coach, supplied the team with gear for the session. We had one of the best training sessions of the season. The players started to joke around about the situation and with each other. The anxiety was dissipating. We called back to OWU and asked the Sports Information Director and women's soccer coach to get all uniforms and soccer shoes from the locker room and bring them down to San Antonio. The mood on the team began to change.

Manage the Money: *Bounce* was a book about business. So, managing the money was a very important part of dealing with adversity. This was not as important to us. The athletics director did provide money to the players who lost everything so they could get a change of clothes, toothbrush, etc.

Manage the Mission: *You lost some things. You will get it all back by Christmas. But you will never have an opportunity to win the national championship again.* This became our mantra. Okay, we have some adversity. But why are we here? We must begin to focus on the soccer side of things. This was difficult for the players, but the team leaders helped the younger players cope. As each hour passed, the focus increased. In fact, we think that this situation helped the team focus. They were angry and worried. They consciously changed their focus from the adversity to the mission.

Manage the Morale: As mentioned earlier, we changed everything. We wanted to make this trip as easy and productive as possible for the players. We upgraded hotel rooms, and we upgraded the places we ate. We created activities (for example, we took a few hours to go to the Alamo) for the players so they would not be sitting around for periods of time and thinking about the problems. We managed every aspect of the weekend!

The results: a 4-1 win over Montclair State in the semi-final game and a 2-1 win over Calvin in the final! Who knows if all these strategies helped us be successful. One of the problems when we make decisions is that we never know if the decision was responsible for the outcome. Would we have won if we did nothing? Or did things differently? Who knows? But the lesson here was how to deal with adversity!

Since the 2011 season, we have adopted a manifest that helps us deal with the "smaller" types of adversity that arise on a day-to-day basis during the season. For example, the team is in a slump and not playing well. This happens in most seasons for a few games. Each player has a three-ring binder in their locker with all kinds of information that they need to be successful during the season. Here is the section on dealing with adversity:

We are going through a rough time. It is normal to have negative thoughts and some self-doubt. That is what a slump is! *But this can be overcome and will be.*

After the second week, I thought we were better than I thought we would be. I thought we were better than last year. *I still think that. We are good and better than last year!*

But we must make some changes. Here are some steps you can take to help us get out of this:

1. **One step at a time:** Don't look too far ahead! Take the first step. Make the next game our best.
2. **Positive self-talk:** Negative thoughts are normal. Self-doubt is normal. Stop the negative thoughts with a cue word and replace with a positive thought.
3. **Positive affirmation:** Write positive affirmations on a 5 x 7 card. i.e., *I am a good soccer player. I am going to work very hard today. I am going to fight like hell today,* etc. Read the positive affirmations before each practice and before each game.
4. **Help and support each other:** This is what a TEAM is all about— each other.

5. **Believe:** Belief is the mother of reality! Have unwavering belief in yourself and the team!
6. **Improve mental strength:** Willpower, desire, determination, and persistence must be exercised just like a muscle must be exercised in every practice. It won't just work for a game.
7. **Past Achievements:** Think about our past successes—how did it feel? Think about our past games—how were you feeling when we were successful?
8. **Push past the pain:** You have not come close to tapping your physical and mental reserves. Fight through it . . .
9. **Focus on the why:** Why were we flat last game? Why did you not play well? What was your state on mind? What was your preparation? What can you do to prepare for the next game? The next practice?

We will get through this!

LESSON VII
EXPERIENCE

"Every experience in your life is being orchestrated to teach you something you need to know to move forward!"
–Brian Tracy

"The most successful people see adversity not as a stumbling block, but as a stepping-stone to greatness."
–Shawn Achor

Experience is the foundation of all knowledge. As coaches, we talk about experience all the time. When we lose a game, we must learn from the experience. Why did we lose? When we win a game, we must learn from that experience. Why did we win? Experience is very powerful and necessary for an organization or team to play at the highest level. Without experience it is not possible to move forward. We always talk about learning from our mistakes. That's experience.

The real definition of experience, then, goes something like this: experience is **the process of living through an event or events. You learn by experience**. Experience is also the skill or knowledge gained by doing a thing—like playing a game. But experience only works if we focus on the experience. Experience does not just happen by playing a game! We must work on it.

What you learn and experience can often **determine success or failure in life and in sport**. Effortful learning combined with real-life on-the-game experience is a winning formula for success. Your choices and your experiences help create the person and player that you are.

But do our players really "gain experience"? Do they really work on experience? Do they even know what experience is? I don't believe they do. They don't work at it. When a game is over, it's over. Let's move on to the next game. Players don't take time to develop or use experience.

Dr. David Cox is a Clinical Psychologist and Associate Professor in the Department of Psychology at Simon Fraser University. He has served as sport psychologist for many sports organizations at both the amateur and professional ranks during the past 15 years. He sees a difference between "athletic performance" and "athletic experience."

Dr Cox worked with several teams and athletes in preparation to compete at the highest level. He became increasingly aware of the distinction between experience and performance at a major athletic competition. He recalled an athlete that he worked with for many years, describing his Olympic experience as "three hundred serious athletes and ten thousand at summer camp." He was making the comparison to the professional tour on which he traveled where the level of commitment was driven by an athlete's knowledge that their livelihood was derived from their performance success. And experience is a key part of performance success. The great NBA player Larry Bird kept a journal in each of the 14 years of his career. In that journal he wrote after each game the reasons he was successful or not that night. He understood the relationship between success and experience.

Dr. Cox continues in his view of this difference, noting that a performance is based on the desire to do all that you can to ensure that you do your best while recognizing that this is independent of the outcome. He suggests that we change our perception of success in athletics. This is a tough concept for athletes to understand. It is not winning or losing that matters; real satisfaction lies in knowing that, regardless of the outcome, you did all that you could to increase the likelihood of success. He suggests that this is a function of competence, or how you feel about yourself, rather than competition, which involves constantly comparing yourself to others. This confidence can be a result of experience, both good and bad.

He feels that experience results simply from having been there. The athletes may indicate that although they enjoyed the experience, they were overwhelmed by it and were not satisfied with their performance. This is true with competition at the highest level. The World Cup, the Super Bowl, college championships—these type of events may lead to being distracted and unable to focus and prepare appropriately for competition. Major events, which are in many ways' festivals of sport, place special demands on athletes and teams to remain very disciplined and manage distractions well, as there may be more of them than is usually experienced in their competitive program. I will say that our 10 trips to the NCAA Division III Soccer Championships added many distractions besides playing the game, so imagine the distractions a World Cup brings. What constitutes a distraction, says Dr. Cox is, of course, an individual matter. There are many issues that can cause problems with athletes, such as location, accommodation, climate, press and media, family and friends, teammates and other athletes, and coaching staff will be experienced in unique ways. The reaction to these "distractions" or experiences is different for each participant. For some, this will be managed well and present minimal distractions and for others it will completely overwhelm them and reduce their readiness to compete.

Dr. Cox goes on to suggest that, for him, this means that major events need to be managed well and athletes need to anticipate, and prepare for, the unique distractions that may be present. This includes accumulating experiences that will help the athlete learn how to handle different situations. If the goal is to produce a best performance, then proper management of the experience will be necessary.

In his mind, Dr. Cox thinks of this in terms of making right choices. Ultimately it is the athlete that must decide how disruptive activities will be. Working to understand experience will help the athlete face the challenges in important competitions at all levels. After all, all coaches want their athletes to come away from important competitions knowing they did the best they could regardless of the outcome.

How can we get our players to think about and use experience? In 2011, the OWU men's soccer team won the national championship. There were eight sophomores who played in that game. Conventional wisdom would suggest that the next 2 years looked good. These players would use the experience they gained in the championship year and lead the team back to the final four. The next two years, we won the conference and the conference tournament but lost in the first round of the NCAA tournament.

I didn't understand how this happened. These players had the experience of winning a national championship but couldn't translate that into a high performance. Then it dawned on me. These players didn't have experience. They should have. But they didn't use the experience of that championship to improve their performance and the team's performance. When the games were over, they were over. There was little or no thought about the lessons learned from the games. The players, in fact, had no experience from the tournament. They played in the games but did not take the time to gain experience.

Since the 2012 season, we have almost forced our players to gain experience from every game. After each game the players send me an email by noon the next day, and they answer the following questions:

As an individual player:

• What went right?
• What went wrong?
• What can I do differently in the next game to improve?

For the team:

• What went right?
• What went wrong?
• What can we do differently in the next game to improve?

At first the players were slow to understand this concept. We had to keep pushing and pushing for the players to send that email. Many just went through the motions and said what they thought the coaching staff wanted to hear. Today it is an accepted and important part of the team culture; the players put some thought into this and actually try to learn from experience.

Here are a few examples from the 2022 season:

PLAYER #1

TEAM EVALUATION

I thought this was one of our best team performances yet. We created a lot of chances, the energy was high, and the score line showed that. Even though we were happy with 4-0, it's great to see we still strive for more goals in games like these. I think we were all happy to see Tyler get a goal and play super well, I thought Ethan Love was excellent today. I still think we force the ball down the right side too much and when we do find the opportunity to switch the ball, we choose not to sometimes. Overall a great team win and we need to keep this up so we have momentum going into post season.

INDIVIDUAL PERFORMANCE

I thought my first half was good, I only lost the ball once or twice in the 25 minutes I played and I created chances for us. I thought I was defending well and switching the ball when I had the chance to. The second half I started really slow the first 20 minutes I was on, taking too many touches and not switching the ball. I had my mind set on getting a goal and I lost my rhythm of the game. When I went in for the last 8 minutes, I started to pick up the rhythm again, creating the chance for Tyler to give the assist to Ethan. I need to keep improving to keep my spot in the starting lineup and get minutes, and I'm still looking for that first goal.

PLAYER #2

Last night was definitely a wake-up call but I don't think it's the end of the world. We were all expecting to win by a decent amount and keep a clean sheet and unfortunately that didn't happen which was a bit of a disappointment. However, I think there were some positive aspects to the game. I thought we moved the ball really well in the second half. I didn't recognize it in the first half, but at halftime Matt and Corey (coaches) put an emphasize on how open the big switch the left wing was. Once I knew to look for it, I was able to play it a couple times and I think it's something that can benefit us in future games. I think defending set pieces was somewhat of an issue because they played it back post and headed it across a couple times which is something we still struggle with. We obviously also could've done a better job of managing the game in the last 10 minutes. I think there were a lot of learning points from this game and we'll be able to improve in future games. Also, my bad for taking my cleats off early on the bench, won't happen again.

PLAYER #3

ABOUT THE TEAM

This was the best game we have played in a long time. Everything was on point. The pre-game warm-up, the energy, the comradery. DePauw didn't have a chance against us and this is how every game should turn out to be. We played like this game was our last. We switched the field, we pressed, we ran, and fought for each other. If we continue to play like this against every team, sky is the limit. One of the things that I liked the most about yesterday is that we had fun. We kind of forgot about having fun during games, and that clearly shows when you play without having fun. I really liked seeing Dante, Tyler, and Justin playing at home. I am excited to see if we can bring this same energy to every single game we have left!

ABOUT ME

I told Matt (coach) before the game that the pre-game warm-up was the best we have had this season. I think this gave me and the team a boost. I combined with Mikey and Griff a couple of times in the first half. I combined and made runs looking for through balls from Hector and Ethan Love. I still have to work on shooting on an empty net and not only just at the net.

PLAYER #4

THINGS I DID WELL

I think today was my best game when it comes to winning the ball out of the air, I was committing to the ball in a way I usually don't, this is something I have been wanting to improve and I am glad to have seen a lot of success in this area.

I went forward at every opportunity, whether that was finding the target's feet or finding the space in behind for our wingers to get onto passes. I would like to find line breaking forward passes more often though.

I defended really well and one of my goals was to win more tackles and win the ball back often, I think I took a big step forward in that regard. It helped us retain possession and that's another part of winning tackles, don't just stop there, find a teammate. I think I did well in that too.

THINGS I CAN WORK ON

I switched the ball maybe twice, I am disappointed because I would catch myself taking it back where it came from, and I always say that's and issue and I need to just commit to getting the ball to the other side no matter what.

I wasn't an option on throw ins enough, that really hurt the team in retaining possession off a throw in, I need to check to the ball quicker to get it back in play quickly.

I had no shots this game, which I am disappointed about. I had it as one of my goals for today and I didn't attempt a single one.

THINGS WE DID WELL
In the first little bit of the first half we were really doing the up back thru well and it was working for us. I think we can continue that pattern of play into finding dangerous passes in behind the defense.

I think there were parts of the first half where we would be dangerous by driving at the defenders, we stopped doing that in the second half but I think we were very creative and direct with our dribbling in the first half.

THINGS WE CAN WORK ON
Holding the ball up, we would finally win the ball back after a while and it would come right back at us, need to learn how to draw a foul or keep hold of it until support arrives.

Along with that, getting up the field quicker is definitely a problem, and I also am part of this. We win the ball back but the work isn't done, we need to step up so we can keep the ball up in their half.

We didn't have a distinct style of play after the first half (generous), we had no identity. I didn't feel for a single minute of the second half we had control over what was happening, I don't remember the last time I had that feeling at OWU.

Most of the players take this seriously. There will always be players who go through the motions. From these examples you can see some things that help the players gain experience:

- They give deep thought to their own performance.
- They recognize the good and bad aspects of their personal performance.
- They make suggestions on how they will get better.
- They recognize teammates who played well.
- They recognize what the team did well and where the team can improve.
- They provide suggestions that can help the team's performance.
- They are making plans for the next game.
- ***They are gaining experience!***

After all the responses are in to my office, I pick 7 to 10 of the best evaluations and send them to the team. Before practice I go over these. That sets the tone for the next few days heading to the next game. This is a big part of our culture. It helps the players take responsibility for their improvement. That is the only way they will get better!

LESSON VIII
COMMUNICATION

"In teamwork, silence isn't golden, it's deadly."
–Mark Sanborn

*"Effective teamwork begins and ends
with communication."*
–Mike Krzyzewski

There is little doubt that good communication will help move a team toward a successful season. Communication adds a great deal to the team culture. And good, open, and honest communication helps the coach establish trust and credibility. Communication, like coaching, is changing. Although most coaches are still control freaks, the *my-way-or-the-highway* or *do-it-because-I-said-so* days are over. Coaches must understand the importance of good communication.

INTERPERSONAL COMMUNICATION

With that said, I will not spend time in this book on interpersonal communication. If necessary, one need only to read the chapter on communication in any sports psychology book. Or even go online to read about:

- The communication processes.
- How to send messages effectively.
- How to receive messages effectively.
- How to identify what causes breakdowns in the communication process.

- How to deal with potential conflict in a sporting environment.
- How to deal with confrontation.
- How to offer constructive criticism.

All these topics are important, very important. But, as mentioned before, are readily available elsewhere. We will focus on the "extra communication" we use at OWU and will show a number of examples we use to facilitate our "extra communication."

Our players all learn differently. Some learn by hearing, some learn by seeing, and some learn kinesthetically. So, it is important that the coach communicates in many ways.

COACH TO PLAYER OR TEAM COMMUNICATION

There is no doubt that communication between the coaching staff and the players is an important factor in team success. Research shows that if athletes know their role on the team and the coach's expectations of them and the team, there is a greater chance of success. Expectations are tricky. If the coach's expectations for the players and the team are unrealistically high, confidence can be negatively impacted. Here, expectations refer to the style of play, the roles in a given formation, the culture of the team, and the expected training habits.

Communicating these to the players is an important part of coaching. It is our belief that this information should be presented in several different ways—verbally and written. We require each player to have a three-ring binder that is kept in their locker. The players are required to keep all handouts in the binder. Handouts include information on the mental aspects of the game and information that covers the expectations. Here are some examples of team expectations:

COACH TO PLAYER/TEAM COMMUNICATION: INTRODUCTION TO OHIO WESLEYAN SOCCER

This is sent to the players in the summer. This introduces the players to several expectations of the program. These address on- and off-the-field expectations. This does not address formations, style of play, and roles of the players.

OHIO WESLEYAN UNIVERSITY SOCCER 2022

I. Why we do what we do

- The combination of academics and soccer exposes and challenges us to develop life skills for the future.
- So, we can achieve our long-term goal: NCAA Soccer Championship.
- So, we can achieve our immediate goals:
  » NCAC Championship
  » NCAA Tournament
- To help you to achieve your personal goals. What are your personal goals? Do you know?

II. OWU Soccer philosophy

- Winning people make wining players who make winning teams,
- Tough soccer challenges in a good soccer environment,
- Play against the best,
- You will be treated like adults/professionals,
- OWU teams *compete* every time we step on the field,
- You will be a *WINNER!*
- Traits of winners: *your mentality, your character, and your lifestyle.*
  » Honesty, trustworthiness, integrity.
  » Passionate.
  » Work ethic every time you step on the field.
  » Dedication to becoming the best student and best soccer player you can be!

- » Coachable—embrace learning.
- » Consistent by playing to your potential every time.
- » Confident.
- » Mental toughness.
- » Humble.
- » Accountable for your actions always, on and off the field.

III. Guidelines for membership on the team

- Make good decisions on and off the field that will give you a chance to be successful.
- Timeliness:
  - » Be on time and be ready to go!
  - » Training is not over until it's over.
- Equipment: we treat you like adults and we expect the same.
  - » Purchase the proper shoes and take care of them.
  - » Wear only OWU practice gear to training.
  - » Wear shin pads always.
  - » Make sure soccer balls are properly inflated and ready to go for each training session.
  - » Help keep the locker room area clean and "always picked up".
  - » Use/wear only YOUR equipment.
  - » No one goes into equipment room.
  - » Freshmen complete all assigned duties.
  - » If you kick a ball out of the field, YOU GO GET IT!
  - » No boxers.
  - » No jewelry.
- Physical:
  - » Proper sleep and eating habits.
  - » Aggressive use of the training staff and weight room to help avoid injuries and rehabilitate injuries.
  - » Proper warm-up and warm down before and after each training session and game.
  - » Report all injuries to the coaching staff and trainer.

- Games:
  - » Wear only OWU-issued game gear.
  - » Use proper bench behavior and decorum—supportive/attentive.
  - » Never create future problems i.e., goal celebrations, trash talk, etc.
  - » Always demonstrate sportsmanship.
  - » Never use bad language!

COACH TO PLAYER/TEAM COMMUNICATION II: WHAT IS GOOD SOCCER? WHAT IS A GOOD PLAYER?

This makes the distinction between our definition of good soccer and bad soccer. This gives the players—who come from many different teams that play different styles of soccer—an understanding of what is acceptable soccer at OWU. The second part presents our definition of a quality player.

OHIO WESLEYAN UNIVERSITY SOCCER 2022

What Is Good Soccer?

Good Soccer	Bad Soccer
1. Play on ground	Played in the air
2. Ball control and accurate	Played first time
3. Frequent and accurate shots	Rare opportunities
4. Shots come from skillfully created openings	Shots come from rebounds and errors
5. Players vary passing and dribbling	Players pass and kick

6. Players make space	Players create no time or space
7. Players have purpose	No purpose or aim
8. Players change position	No movement
9. Players use skill	Players foul and intimidate
10. Defenders mark, cover, and tackle fairly	Late hits, yellow cards, and violent tackles
11. Players play for each other	Players play for themselves
12. Players use positive communication	Players whine and curse
13. Players come off the field physically exhausted	Players come off the field with something left
14. Players are confident	Players are afraid to make mistakes
15. Players make good and quick decisions	Players are slow with decision making
16. Players are creative	Players are predictable
17. Players want to get better	Players are content with their level of play
18. Players have fun	The game becomes work

What Is a Quality Player?

1. A definition:

- He/She has sensitive touch and tight control . . . can you receive the ball under pressure?
- Can you make space/time for yourself?
- Are you deceptive?
- Can you get "out of trouble?"
- Can you combine with a player? With a third player?

2. Do you "have a game?"

- Do you play for yourself or for others? Can you do both if necessary?
- Do you create problems without the ball?
- Can you free yourself from tight markers? Can you free others?
- Do you react to play or are you a move or two ahead of the play?
- Are you farsighted or nearsighted?

3. What are the physical attributes?

- Do you have fluid movement?
- Do you have good agility?
- Do you have a good change of pace?
- Can you produce a high level of work and sustain it over time?
- Do you use athletic ability, or do you depend upon it?
- Are you strong in 1v1 situations?

4. What kind of competitor are you?

- Can you impose your will on opponents?
- How do you react to intimidation?
- How do you react to dirty play?

- Do you have physical and moral courage?
- How tough minded are you?
- How do you react to losing?

*These indicate two biases I have of American soccer players. In my mind, too many games and too many tournaments contribute to this. Our players do not change pace, AND they rely on their athletic ability rather than use it!

COACH TO PLAYER/TEAM COMMUNICATION III

Do you want to communicate something to a smaller group of players than the entire team. Do so verbally and follow with a handout like this:

Expectations of the Leaders by the Coach
1. **Honesty:** When asked a question, when you give an opinion.
2. **Effort:** Lead by example . . . be the first in everything.
3. **Positive Attitude:** When things are tough, teammates will look to you to follow. If you are positive, they will be positive.
4. **Don't Change:** Be yourself . . . be true to your convictions . . . be you.
5. **Goal Oriented:** Keep your eye on the prize—know where we are going; setbacks are not a problem, but losing our way is a problem.
6. **One Mind:** We can disagree—and I expect you to say what you have to say about anything—but when we walk on the field, we are ONE.
7. **Responsible:** Do what is necessary and accept responsibility.
8. **Dependable:** Do what you say you will with coach or teammate.
9. **Disciplined:** Do what has to be done, when it has to be done, and do it the best you possibly can.
10. **Have Fun:** When it ain't fun, get out!

COACH TO PLAYER/TEAM COMMUNICATION IV: INSPIRATIONAL PIECE THAT WE SEND TO PLAYERS IN THE SUMMER AND THROUGHOUT THE SEASON

These deal primarily with the mental side of the game.

Ohio Wesleyan University Soccer 2022

You Gotta Believe . . .

> *"The biggest thing is to have a mindset and a belief*
> *that you can win every tournament going in..."*
>
> *–Tiger Woods*

> *"When you believe in yourself and in the people,*
> *you surround yourself with, you will win something*
> *really big someday . . ."*
>
> *–Dick Vermeil, NFL coach*

I attended a large college ID Camp a few years ago, I saw a lot of good players, and I saw the Wake Forest team play twice. I was struck with the reality that they are very good. I was also struck by the fact that most of you could play for Wake Forest. They have two "special players"—a defensive midfielder and a center back—but most of their players are just like **you!** The difference? They **believe** they are good. You **hope** you are good or maybe not bad.

Belief is a state or habit of the mind in which trust or confidence is placed in some person or something. Beliefs drive behavior, and behavior affects performance in everything we do. Many of you do not believe that you are good. You are. You would not be here if you were not good. You must learn to have trust in your talent. You must learn to believe in yourself when under pressure. You must expect to be successful—notice I didn't say win. I said successful—to me, success means working hard and being relentless.

In psychology there is a term called self-efficacy. It is the belief in one's own ability to be successful. However, simply believing in yourself does not mean you will win every game. But believing in yourself can put you in a position to win. Nick Saban, a successful American football coach, said, "You've got to believe deep inside yourself that you are destined to do great things."

Belief systems are a big part of confidence. On the other hand, beliefs that are irrational or unrealistic lead to stress. Let's look at the **ABC Theory** of success and stress.

The **A** stands for the activating event: *a soccer game against Denison.* The **B** is your belief about the event: *I have worked hard in training; I am prepared mentally and physically for this game; I am going out on the field and play well.* The **C** stands for consequences, the feelings, and behaviors about the outcome: *I played a good game, I played smart, I was aggressive, I had a good game.*

There are many unrealistic or irrational beliefs you may have about yourself. Some of you think you are not technical enough, fast enough, smart enough, or good enough to play at a high level. *Where is the evidence?* Some of you have a belief system that says failure is a shameful thing. In truth, life is based on failure—if you believed that failure was terrible, you never would have learned to walk! Do you know which NBA player missed the most game-winning shots in NBA history? Michael Jordan. Do you know which NBA player holds the record for making the most game-winning shots in NBA history? Michael Jordan. Larry Bird (I had to get him in here) is second in both categories. They are two pretty good players.

Another irrational belief is: *If I mess up, no one will like me. I'll be rejected.* That kind of thinking puts enormous stress on you. If you believe that by not winning, you are a loser, that by losing, no one will like you, that taking a risk is dangerous, and that not being perfect is unacceptable, you will be under stress and have problems in life! And that stress will adversely affect your performance.

One way to counter irrational beliefs is with positive affirmation (i.e., positive self-talk). These affirmations should be positive, powerful, and in the present. Muhammad Ali was a master of positive affirmation: *"It's a lack of faith that makes people afraid of meeting challenges, **and I believed in myself!**"* Or *"To be a great champion, you must believe that you are the best. If you're not, pretend you are."* Or *"I'm so mean I make medicine sick!"* Finally, *"There are only two Greats in this world – Britain and me."*

Do you believe in yourself? Ask yourself that question. What is your belief system? Do you believe in your dreams? Your goals? Your ability?

What your mind can conceive and what your heart believes, you can achieve . . .

Beliefs drive behaviors and self-limiting beliefs lead to self-defeating behaviors. Believe in yourself. Believe in your abilities. Believe in your teammates.

COACH TO PLAYER/TEAM COMMUNICATION V

Another example of expectations for the players. This is very clear. *These are the coach's expectations of you at training.*

OHIO WESLEYAN UNIVERSITY SOCCER 2022
TRAINING HABITS

MENTAL ATTITUDE

- Know that events of the day can influence training.
- Be on time.
- Be ready to play.
- Be passionate.
- Have pride in everyday performance.
- Be coachable.

- Be a leader.
- Be positive.
- Be the best player at each training session i.e., focused, hard work, etc.

BODY LANGUAGE

- Be positive.
- Eye contact.
- Posture.
- Jog in when called by coach.

EQUIPMENT

- Only OWU gear.
- Clean shoes.
- Jersey tucked in at all times.
- Socks and shin guards.
- No jewelry.
- Inflate all soccer balls for every practice.

PHYSICAL

- Proper eating and sleeping.
- Use the training room and weight room.
- Proper warm-up and warm down.

PLAY IN TRAINING

- Be hard—but be honest in effort.
- No fouls! Why foul teammate? Why hurt teammate?
- Swearing is a foul and yellow card!
- React to whistle—freeze/stop.
- No dissent—verbal or nonverbal.

REACTION TO CRITICISM

- Remember it is helping you to get better.
- Eye contact with coach during discussion.
- Acknowledge the comment.
- Think! How could you have helped the situation.
- Smile—you are learning!

DISCUSSION/QUESTIONS

- Do not stop session to discuss options—ask coach at break or after practice.
- If explanations are not clear—ask away!
- If you foul teammate—help him up.
- Help with field and equipment set up.

PAY ATTENTION—you will learn faster and play more!

COACH TO PLAYER COMMUNICATION VI

This piece is very specific for the players and for each position. When players know their role, they have a chance to play at a higher level. We talk about these roles constantly. With this piece, the players can see exactly what is expected.

OHIO WESLEYAN MEN'S SOCCER POSITIONAL RESPONSIBILITIES/DUTIES

FULL BACK (#2/3)
The full back is a key player in modern soccer, having to supplement his traditional defensive duties with overlapping runs down the wing to support forward play and help overload attacks in the final third.

Although primarily a defensive player, he must be prepared to get forward when the team needs extra width.

Defend
Stay with the defensive lines and make simple short passes down the flank or into the central midfield.

- Active player instructions
  - » Fewer risky passes
  - » Hold position

Support
Support the midfield by providing extra width and look for crosses and through balls when the opportunity arises.

- Active player instructions
  - » Cross from deep

Attack
Supplements his/her defensive responsibilities by overlapping the midfield and providing first time crosses into the area.

- Active player instructions
  - » Cross more often, get further forward

CENTRAL DEFENDER (#4/5)
The main job of the central defender is to stop the opposing attackers from playing and to clear the ball from danger when required.

However, especially for more aggressive tactics, he/she must also possess the technique and composure to be able to help the team maintain possession and lay off simple passes to more creative players.

Defend

The central defender will stay in line with his defensive partner and look to break up attacks, mark opposing forwards, and prevent the ball from getting into the box.

- Active player instructions
    - » Shoot less often
    - » Dribble less
    - » Fewer risky passes
    - » Hold position

CENTRAL MIDFIELDER

The central midfielder is responsible for providing an industrious and versatile link between the defense and attack. Expected to perform a variety of tasks across the center of the field, the central midfielder benefits from having the tactical awareness and technical ability to support both defensive and attacking play as needed.

Defend (#6)

The central midfielder will focus more on sitting deep, curtailing opposition counter attacks, and controlling the tempo of the game from the center of the field.

- Active player instructions
    - » Hold position
    - » Close down more

Support (#8)

The central midfielder will look to balance his attacking and defensive responsibilities. He will get forward when necessary, but he will mainly keep the center of the field and attempt to thread passes to players in the final third.

- Active player instructions
  - » None

Attack (#10)
The central midfielder will more readily surge into the final third to support the forwards around the box.

- Active player instructions
  - » Get further forward

WINGERS (#7/11)
The winger aims to beat his opponent on the outside and needs to be technically proficient as well as quick in order to do so.

The winger hugs the touchline when the team is going forward, ready to surge into space and attack the byline.

Support
The winger's job is to try to quickly get past his opponent and get in an early cross to the forwards

- Active player instructions
  - » Dribble more
  - » Run wide with the ball
  - » Cross more often
  - » Stay wider

Attack
The winger will try and run at the defense in the final third, aiming to cause panic and indecision prior to shooting or attempting to make a through ball/cross to teammate.

- Active player instructions
  - » Dribble more
  - » Run wide with the ball
  - » Cross more often
  - » Stay wider
  - » Cross from byline
  - » Get further forward

STRIKER (#9)

The target player uses physicality to disrupt the opposition's defense and open space for his striker partner and supporting midfielders.

The target player uses strength and aerial presence to bring teammates into play rather than relying on technical ability.

Support

The target player will look to win flick-ons and play simple possession passes to teammates to bring them into play.

- Active player instructions
  - » Hold up ball
  - » Dribble less

Attack

The target player will lead the line and open space for teammates to move into.

- Active player instructions
  - » Hold up ball
  - » Dribble less
  - » Get further forward

Communication is also important between the coaching staff. All coaches must know exactly what their role is on the coaching team and what direction the team is going.

Communication to Coaches I
Knowing what is expected by coaches is important.

OHIO WESLEYAN UNIVERSITY SOCCER 2022
MARTIN'S MANIFESTO TO THE COACHING STAFF

Vision
- We will have a talented and deep team that is intelligent and hardworking, efficient in scoring and defending, competing on a national level.

Targets
- Use preseason/scrimmages to identify the best formation and depth chart for the fall season.
- Use the non-conference schedule to identify the true potential for the team, preparing them for the most important phase—conference play.
- Use the previous targets to identify what we need to do to get results in conference play.

We will improve the image of the program by:

- Focusing on team development over anything else.
- Improving the players' motivation to buy-in to the we-versus-me mindset.
- Improving the "sweep the shed" ownership of the players.
- Eliminating negativity and issues as soon as they arise.

We will create a learning environment by:

- Maximizing the we present information (pre-training meetings, white board, film, meetings).
- Optimizing the elements of the training activities (always connected to the game and game model), avoiding doing activities that are just "good" for the sake of looking good.
- Clear objectives and goals in training and valuing player/team feedback.

We will recruit better talent by:

- Attending multiple games and tournaments where players are "showcased'
- By using alums to identify talent
- By using high school coaches we have worked with in the past
- By using our current players as resources to identify good players they may know

We will improve our communication by:

- You and I just need to make sure we go over things together, so whether we are being asked something together or separately, the message is the same.
- Using a leadership group more often to discuss feedback/issues that we may not be fully aware of, for example, Ethan Love can't stand playing with Hector and Cristian . . .

We will build winning attitudes by:

- Optimizing competition in training.
- Rewarding effort, focus, leadership.
- Zero tolerance for excuses, blaming, etc.

We will improve the physical capabilities of our players by:

- Using the Beyond Pulse data to monitor rest/recovery.
- Always having a proper warm-up and cool-down.
- Lifting during the season (for maintenance).
- Tracking player health, sleep, etc.

We will improve the technical abilities of our players by:

- Maximizing touches in activities . . . train with the ball as much as we can.
- Functional and facilitating things for the guys to do before/after training.

Our three key systems of play (general, defending a lead, chasing the game) will be:

- General: value possession, but the focus is always getting in behind, combination play, numerical superiority, pressing and defending safe.
- Defending a lead: killing the clock, minimizing risk, still focusing on scoring if it arises.
- Chasing a game: speed of play, taking chances, still mindful of defending.

These are the key ways we will score:

- Always have numbers in the box.
- Timing of crosses/runs.
- Getting the ball in behind early and often (we can press to create chances as well).
- Set pieces.
- Individual talent.

We will prevent goals by:

- Having an organized and disciplined back line.
- Having a team commitment to defending.
- Being excellent in restart defense.
- Limiting shots, crosses, and fouls.

We will coach set pieces by:

- Have a playbook that is practiced in various forms consistently in training.
- I rarely prioritize set pieces but 30% of goals come from them!

We will teach transition by:

- Including it in as many activities as possible.
- Taking pride in outworking opponents in transition moments.

Our policy for dealing with setbacks will be:

- Staying positive and looking forward.
- Reflecting on how to improve and set a plan to get there.

Our game plan to the team consists of:

- Projected formation, set pieces, match-ups.
- Present things from the perspective of how we will be successful instead of focusing on what the opponent will do.

Our priorities managing game day will be:

- Maintaining our pre-game routine(s).
- Making sure all operations are set.
- Making sure players expect to play and know our tactics and their roles.

We will help the team pre-match by:

- Being organized and confident.
- Meeting the players' needs, questions, concerns.
- Preparing them to be successful.

We will deal with results by:

- Recapping the positives.
- Focusing on the process and improvement—there will be bumps.

We learn from each game by:

- Film review.
- Revisiting our game goals and tactics.
- Answer the "why"?

Our players are held accountable by:

- Receiving feedback with actual data.
- Editing/revising goals and training plans.

Preseason goals include:

Maximizing 11v11:

- We need to train how we will play as early and often as possible.
- We can build endurance fitness through 11v11.
- We can focus on the larger principles before we get more specific.

Simplicity:

- Everything relates to the game.
- Don't need to have many exercises per session.
- Repeated activities but with a different focus.
- Coaching points always related to the main topics, nothing else!

Competition:

- Most activities
  - » Have a way to score.
  - » Have transition.
  - » Are competitive.
  - » Have a technical and tactical goal.
  - » Are realistic.
  - » Are simple, progressive, challenging, and fun.

These examples take communication to the next level. Not only do we tell the players what is expected, but we show them and present handouts like these to reinforce expectations. Players and coaches need more than being **told** what to do. They need to be **shown** what to do. The more methods of communication, the better chance of success. Improve your communication!

LESSON IX
THE LITTLE THINGS

"The philosophy of 'Don't sweat the small stuff?'
Yeah, that was never his philosophy."
–Jim Swartz to Bill Belichick

"If you think small things don't matter, think of the
last game you lost by one point."
–Anonymous

Do you know what the difference is between good teams, players, or organizations and great teams, players, or organizations? The great ones do the little things. The great ones do little things that other teams or players either can't do, or more likely, won't do. Players don't change when they walk on the field. If they don't do the little things off the field, they won't do the little things on the field! It is simple. And little things equate to big success.

For example, if I see a player walk past a piece of trash without picking it up, we have a problem. What is the player thinking? *I don't have to pick up trash, let someone else pick it up!* In the game, that same player will not track back 50 yards to defend. *I don't have to defend, let someone else defend!* It's the little things that make a huge difference.

In my experience, many incoming freshmen have trouble with this concept. They are all good players in club or high school. They didn't have to do the little things to make themselves and the team better. Someone else covered for them. Often, early in the season when we are moving goals or picking up the gear, these players "hide." They let someone else do the work. That must be stopped immediately. It happens every year.

This chapter is about the little things that we do in the OWU program that most programs don't, can't, or won't do. And it offers some ideas about the little things in the game of soccer on and off the field.

My current assistant tells this story about his first year with the program.

"We lost 4-1 to a big rival. We didn't play well. After the game I was shocked because he did not talk about the game. He told the team they were not doing the job in the locker room. The sinks were dirty from washing cleats. The trash had not been emptied. The floor was a mess. The players lockers were unkempt. We were not doing the little things that create success. Just like the locker room, we did not do the little things on the field to be successful. He told the players that *you don't change when you walk on the field. If you don't do the little things off the field, you won't do them on the field!* They got the point. The locker room was cleaned and kept clean for the rest of the season and we immediately won 10 in a row! The little things are important!"

THE POWER OF PLEASE AND THANK YOU

The coaching staff and players never tell each other what to do. We always say please and thank you. *Ok guys, please help me move the goals. Thanks.* Often the coaching staff will help move the goals. This shows the team we are all in this together. The coaching staff is not autocratic. If we demonstrate working together, the trust and credibility of the staff is enhanced. The coaching staff help with all the chores. We wash clothes. Sweep the floor. Pick up the gear. We are all in this together.

Fergus Connelly in his book *Game Changer* talks about the little things. When the whistle blows to start a soccer game, chaos immediately ensues. The outcome of the game can turn on one single event in 90 minutes. A missed penalty kick. A shot over the goal. A bad decision on a breakaway. A game can turn on any of those things. Coaches look at the outcome of a game and can only guess at why the outcome was what it was. The game is too complex to see if one event caused the result.

Focusing on the little things off the field will help the players develop a "little things mindset." Make sure the serve on a corner kick is perfect. Look before you get the ball to help improve decision making. When a teammate makes a bad pass to you, simply give a thumbs up and a *my bad* comment.

Similarly, we never call players by their last name. Or even by a nickname. We respect the players as good human beings who happen to be playing soccer. Do you like to be called by your last name? A nickname? I don't think so. So, we don't do it. The little things.

This all developed because of my leadership philosophy. I was a boy scout. An eagle scout, of course. But the only thing I remember from scouts (it was a long time ago), was the first page in the *Boy Scout Handbook* in the chapter on leadership. There were two pictures on top of the chapter heading. Both pictures showed four boy scouts. One was clearly the leader. The other three were followers. In the first picture, the leader pointed and said, *"Go get some wood."* In the second picture, the leader said, *"Let's go get some wood!"* "Let's" is a contraction for "let us." I have never forgotten that. We are in this together. Thank you.

NON-NEGOTIABLE STANDARDS

We have talked a lot about empowerment and relationships with players and how that impacts the team and helps move us toward a successful season. We are not suggesting that the coaching staff have no input into the program at all. We lead. We guide. We empower. We oversee the program and make sure we are heading in the right direction.

Although we allow the players to set the values and standards, we do have some non-negotiable standards that have been the foundation of the program for 45 years. You too should have these non-negotiable standards. Here are some examples of non-negotiable standards:

- Attendance
- Timeliness

- Respect for all
- Drug- and alcohol-related standards
- Accountability
- Responsibility
- Self-discipline
- Trustworthiness

And there are many more to choose from. At OWU we have only two non-negotiable standards:

- Act first class on and off the field.
- Do not do anything to embarrass yourself, the team, or Ohio Wesleyan.

These two do not need definition. We all know what they mean! We also use the standards from Bill Walsh's book. Walsh was a coach for the American Football team, the San Francisco 49ers. He inherited a terrible team and managed to create a dynasty winning multiple Super Bowls. Here are his standards for performance:

- Exhibit a ferocious and intelligently applied work ethic directed toward continual improvement.
- Demonstrate respect for each person in the organization and the work he or she does.
- Be deeply committed to learning and teaching, which means increasing our own expertise.
- Be fair.
- Demonstrate character.
- Honor the direct connection between details and improvement.
- Relentlessly seek improvement.
- Show self-control, especially when it counts most—under pressure.
- Demonstrate and prize loyalty.
- Use positive language and have a positive attitude.
- Take pride in my effort as an entity separate from the results of that effort.

- Be willing to go the extra distance for the organization.
- Deal appropriately with victory and defeat, adulation, and humiliation.
- Promote internal communication that is both open and substantive (especially under stress).
- Seek poise in myself and those I lead.
- Put the team's welfare and priorities ahead of my own.
- Maintain an ongoing level of concentration and focus that is abnormally high.
- Make sacrifice and commitment the organization's trademark.
- The leader must exhibit the principles, code of conduct, and behavior that he is asking others to emulate.

Although Bill Walsh was an NFL coach, we can all learn and apply some, if not all, of his standards. Some food for thought.

GERMANY I

When I arrived at OWU, there was no place for our players to watch good soccer. I moved from Germany, a soccer culture, to the US, which had no soccer culture. Our players did not have role models to watch every weekend like they do today. I had German friends send video of Bundesliga games so the players could see what good soccer looked like. Changing the tape to American video became very expensive!

I decided it would be better to go to Germany and play against German teams. We have been to Germany 13 times since 1980. We play against a variety of German teams on each trip. We want to introduce our team to the whole spectrum of German soccer. We play against lowest level "town teams" in small towns and against Bundesliga A-Jugend (Youth) teams. We usually play against FC Bayern's U19s and Schalke U10s. We have contacts at each of these clubs and have played them many times. We also get a Bundesliga game or two in and, if lucky, the German Super Cup. The Super Cup pits last year's Bundesliga champion against the cup winner. For two weeks the guys are immersed into a "soccer culture"!

But it is more than a soccer trip. It is a cultural trip as well. Years ago, a former OWU player went to a small German town called Baumholder. He played on the town team for two seasons. When he returned to the United States, he became my assistant coach. He suggested that we go to Baumholder on the next trip and stay with German families. Baumholder is ideally situated near Kaiserslautern. From there we go south to München and Nürnberg. Come back to Baumholder and go north to Gelsenkirchen (Schalke 04) and Düsseldorf or Köln. It works out great and the players get to meet real German families. Many of our players stay in touch with "their family." When Germany hosted the 2006 World Cup, 19 players came to Baumholder to stay with "their family" before going to games!

This trip has become part of our team's culture. Only one class has missed a trip (Covid-19). The trip is a common denominator that holds alumni together!

GERMANY II

In June of 1971 I moved to Munich, Germany (and later Düsseldorf) to play basketball. Yes, basketball, I was never any good at soccer. But this move to Munich opened my eyes to soccer. Germany has a soccer-based sports culture. Bayern Munich was, for all intents and purposes, the German National Team-Die Mannschaft. Maier, Beckenbauer, Schwarzenbeck, Kapellmann, Hoeneß, Müller, among others, all played at Bayern and for the World Cup winning 1974 team.

My basketball playing and coaching job did not start until late afternoon. I lived in northern Munich. The Bayern and 1860 training grounds were in southern Munich. Every morning I would take the tram south to the Bayern or 1860 training ground. I watched training and really got into soccer. After a month or two I noticed another man at every practice. Over time we got to talking to each other and became friends. It turns out he was Helmut Schön. At the time, the national team coach of Germany. In one of our discussions, he told me how to put a team together in soccer.

He said there are three types of players:

- The personality player: A player who puts his stamp on the game. You walk out of the stadium and think about the contribution they made.
- The creative player: I call these players pink shirts. They have a high level of creativity and are necessary for every team. Maybe they don't defend or run as much as you would like, but they are important to the team.
- The fighter: I call these players dirt bags. They do all the dirty work for the team. The shirts are stained in warm-ups. These players are necessary too.

The rules:

- If you are lucky enough to have two personality players, do not play them side by side. They will both "take away" the play from each other.
- Play a fighter next to every creative player. The fighter will do the dirty work for the creative player.
- Spread the creative players around the field. That ensures different opportunities from different spots on the field.

My first team at OWU had two personality players. And a lot of good players to ensure a good season. Being the young coach who knew it all, I started the year in a 4-2-4. The two personality players were in the midfield. I thought, with their great ability, they would control midfield, and we would be fine. We started out 0-3-3, the longest non-winning streak we have ever had. Then I remembered what Helmut Schön told me. I put one of the personality players at sweeper and one at the attacking midfield spot. We switched to a 4-3-3 and won 123 games in a row. Your players and the coach should do what they can do . . . only!

THE MENTAL

This book is about creating a culture that will last and help the team play at the highest level. I have not presented tactics, techniques, or fitness material. You can find that stuff anywhere. But a quick word about the mental. I have touched on the mental a few times in this book. The chapters on values, goal setting, adversity, and communication all touched on the mental. I am not going into detail here about what we do for the mental. Because we do a lot. As the players move up from what I call the athletics pyramid from youth, to college, to pros, the mental becomes more important.

We focus on the following psychological attributes with the team. This starts in the summer and continues through the entire season. We work on the following:

- Positive self-talk
- Goal setting
- Performance routines
- Imagery
- Energy control
- Attention and focus
- Emotional control
- Confidence

I am not going to spend time here talking about this. You can find information on these attributes in a sports psych book. But I do want to share two instruments that we use for mental aspects.

The first is a Psychological Performance Inventory. This was first created by Dr. James Loehr in the late 1990s. It measures seven psychological attributes. We give this to the players in preseason. It helps the players evaluate their strengths and weaknesses psychologically. After the evaluation, the players know where they need work.

PSYCHOLOGICAL PERFORMANCE INVENTORY

Questions:

1. I see myself as more of a loser than a winner in competition.

1	2	3	4	5
Almost Always	Often	Sometimes	Seldom	Almost Never

2. I get angry and frustrated during competition.

1	2	3	4	5
Almost Always	Often	Sometimes	Seldom	Almost Never

3. I become distracted and lose my focus during competition.

1	2	3	4	5
Almost Always	Often	Sometimes	Seldom	Almost Never

4. Before competition, I picture myself performing perfectly.

1	2	3	4	5
Almost Always	Often	Sometimes	Seldom	Almost Never

5. I am highly motivated to play at my best.

1	2	3	4	5
Almost Always	Often	Sometimes	Seldom	Almost Never

6. I can keep strong positive emotion flowing during competition.

1	2	3	4	5
Almost Always	Often	Sometimes	Seldom	Almost Never

7. I am a positive thinker during competition.

1	2	3	4	5
Almost Always	Often	Sometimes	Seldom	Almost Never

8. I believe in myself as a player.

1	2	3	4	5
Almost Always	Often	Sometimes	Seldom	Almost Never

9. I get nervous or afraid in competition.

1	2	3	4	5
Almost Always	Often	Sometimes	Seldom	Almost Never

10. It seems my mind starts racing 100 mph during critical moments of competition.

1	2	3	4	5
Almost Always	Often	Sometimes	Seldom	Almost Never

11. I mentally practice my physical skills.

1	2	3	4	5
Almost Always	Often	Sometimes	Seldom	Almost Never

12. The goals I've set for myself as a player keep me working hard.

1	2	3	4	5
Almost Always	Often	Sometimes	Seldom	Almost Never

13. I am able to enjoy competition even when I face lots of difficult problems.

1	2	3	4	5
Almost Always	Often	Sometimes	Seldom	Almost Never

14. My self-talk during competition is negative.

1	2	3	4	5
Almost Always	Often	Sometimes	Seldom	Almost Never

15. I lose my confidence very quickly.

1	2	3	4	5
Almost Always	Often	Sometimes	Seldom	Almost Never

16. Mistakes get me feeling and thinking negatively.

1	2	3	4	5
Almost Always	Often	Sometimes	Seldom	Almost Never

17. I can clear interfering emotions quickly and regain my focus.

1	2	3	4	5
Almost Always	Often	Sometimes	Seldom	Almost Never

18. Thinking in pictures about my sport comes easy for me.

1	2	3	4	5
Almost Always	Often	Sometimes	Seldom	Almost Never

19. I don't have to be pushed to play or practice hard. I am my own best igniter.

1	2	3	4	5
Almost Always	Often	Sometimes	Seldom	Almost Never

20. I tend to get emotionally flat when things turn against me during play.

1	2	3	4	5
Almost Always	Often	Sometimes	Seldom	Almost Never

21. I give 100 percent effort during play, no matter what.

1	2	3	4	5
Almost Always	Often	Sometimes	Seldom	Almost Never

22. I can perform toward the upper range of my talent and skill.

1	2	3	4	5
Almost Always	Often	Sometimes	Seldom	Almost Never

23. My muscles become overly tight during competition.

1	2	3	4	5
Almost Always	Often	Sometimes	Seldom	Almost Never

24. I get spacey during competition.

1	2	3	4	5
Almost Always	Often	Sometimes	Seldom	Almost Never

25. I visualize working through tough situations prior to competition.

1	2	3	4	5
Almost Always	Often	Sometimes	Seldom	Almost Never

26. I'm willing to give whatever it takes to reach my full potential as a player.

1	2	3	4	5
Almost Always	Often	Sometimes	Seldom	Almost Never

27. I practice with high positive intensity.

1	2	3	4	5
Almost Always	Often	Sometimes	Seldom	Almost Never

28. I can change negative moods into positive ones by controlling my thinking.

1	2	3	4	5
Almost Always	Often	Sometimes	Seldom	Almost Never

29. I'm a mentally tough competitor.

1	2	3	4	5
Almost Always	Often	Sometimes	Seldom	Almost Never

30. Uncontrollable events like the wind, cheating opponents, and bad referees get me very upset.

1	2	3	4	5
Almost Always	Often	Sometimes	Seldom	Almost Never

31. I find myself thinking of past mistakes or missed opportunities as I play.

1	2	3	4	5
Almost Always	Often	Sometimes	Seldom	Almost Never

32. I use images during play that help me perform better.

1	2	3	4	5
Almost Always	Often	Sometimes	Seldom	Almost Never

33. I get bored and burned out.

1	2	3	4	5
Almost Always	Often	Sometimes	Seldom	Almost Never

34. I get challenged and inspired in tough situations.

1	2	3	4	5
Almost Always	Often	Sometimes	Seldom	Almost Never

35. My coaches would say I have a good attitude.

1	2	3	4	5
Almost Always	Often	Sometimes	Seldom	Almost Never

36. I project the outward image of a confident fighter.

1	2	3	4	5
Almost Always	Often	Sometimes	Seldom	Almost Never

37. I can remain calm during competition when confused by problems.

1	2	3	4	5
Almost Always	Often	Sometimes	Seldom	Almost Never

38. My concentration is easily broken.

1	2	3	4	5
Almost Always	Often	Sometimes	Seldom	Almost Never

39. When I visualize myself playing, I can see and feel things vividly.

1	2	3	4	5
Almost Always	Often	Sometimes	Seldom	Almost Never

40. I wake up in the morning and am really excited about playing and practicing.

1	2	3	4	5
Almost Always	Often	Sometimes	Seldom	Almost Never

41. Playing this sport gives me a genuine sense of joy and fulfillment.

1	2	3	4	5
Almost Always	Often	Sometimes	Seldom	Almost Never

42. I can turn crisis into opportunity.

1	2	3	4	5
Almost Always	Often	Sometimes	Seldom	Almost Never

How to Score the Results

If you will go back and look, you will see a number circled for each item. Take that number and place it alongside the item number in the following chart.

Self Confidence	Negative Energy	Attention Control	Visual Imagery and Control	Motivational Level
1.	2.	3.	4.	5.
8.	9.	10.	11.	12.
15.	16.	17.	18.	19.
22.	23.	24.	25.	26.
29.	30.	31.	32.	33.
36.	37.	38.	39.	40.
Total	Total	Total	Total	Total

Positive Energy		Attitude Control	
6.		7.	
13.		14.	

20.	21.
27.	28.
34.	35.
41.	42.
Total	Total

After doing this for all 42 items, add each of the seven columns separately. Use that total for making your own profile of mental strengths and weaknesses. Any of your total scores that fall below 20 need your special attention. When that happens, thoroughly review all training procedures that relate to that area of weakness.

26–30	Excellent Skills
20–25	Room for Improvement
6–19	Needs Your Special Attention

The second instrument is called Competition Reflections. The idea is to have the players answer the questions on both pages. They are asked to remember the best game they ever played. What were they thinking? How did they feel? What was the energy level? Then they are asked to remember the worst game they ever played. The idea is for the players to replicate their feelings before each game so they feel the same way they did before the best game they ever played. Players love this. This gives them an opportunity to strive toward being mentally prepared for each game. Not just showing up and hoping they are ready to play.

COMPETITION REFLECTIONS
These questions are designed to help you reflect upon your personal competitive history and to help you develop or refine a pre-competition plan and a competition focus plan.

Knowing your competition self

1. Think of your all-time best performance(s) and respond to the following questions keeping that event(s) in mind:

On a scale of 0 to 10, how did you feel just before that event? 0 = no activation (mentally and physically flat); 10 = highly activated (mentally and physically charged)

On a scale of 0 to 10, were you not worried or scared at all (=0) or extremely worried or scared (=10)?

2. What were you saying to yourself or thinking shortly before the start of the event(s)?

3. How were you focused during the event (i.e., what were you aware of or paying attention to while actively engaged in the performance)?

4. Now think of your worst competitive performance(s) and respond to the following questions keeping that event in mind:

On a scale of 0-10, how did you feel just before that event? 0 = no activation (mentally and physically flat); 10 = highly activated (mentally and physically charged

On a scale of 0-10, were you not worried or scared at all (=0) or extremely worried or scared (=10)?

5. What were you saying to yourself or thinking shortly before the start of that event?

6. How were you focused during the event (i.e., what were you aware of or paying attention to while actively engaged in the performance)?

7. What were the major differences between your thinking (or feelings) prior to these two performances (i.e., best and worst)?

8. What were the major differences in your focus of attention during these performances (i.e., best and not-so-best)?

9. On a scale of 0-10, how would you prefer to feel just before an important performance? 0 = no activation (mentally and physically flat); 10 = highly activated (mentally and physically charged)
10. How would you prefer to focus your attention during an important performance?

11. Is there anything you would like to change about the way you approach a competition? Or training?

12. Is there anything you would prefer to change about the way the coach approaches you during training or competitions?

These two instruments will get you started with the mental side of the game. Please note, these are a part of the player's self-evaluation. The players cannot get better if they don't know where they are!

Players should know what they can and cannot do. When they play in a game, **they should only do what they can do.** Players should not try something new in a game. But they all do. Their heart is in the right place—they are trying to help the team. But most often they do, or try to do, exactly what they should not do. **Players should try things in practice, not games.** In practice we encourage trying new things and want the players to make mistakes. That is how they learn. Mistakes in games lead to a loss of confidence and the level of play goes down! This is a tough lesson.

My example comes from the NBA. Michael Jordan had an enormous skill set. Larry Bird did not have such a large skill set. Yet, both are considered all-time greats in NBA history.

Why? Because Larry Bird did not try to be like Mike. He knew what he could do and that's what he did. That is all he did. But they both did well.

WHEN IS THE BEST TIME TO CHANGE THINGS UP?

Things aren't going well. The team is struggling. They have lost a few games in a row. It means time to make changes.

No. That is exactly when you should not make changes. In my experience, when you make these changes, you are "piling on the team" in a negative way. The players already have some self-doubt. They are struggling with a lack of confidence. By making changes you send the message that we really are not good. Why should we add to the downward spiral?

The time to make changes is when things are going well. After we won our second national championship in 2011, my assistant and I changed everything about the program:

- How we recruit.
- Who we recruit.
- How we find talent.
- How we add to our personal development.
- How we train.
- What we train—we changed how we present information to the team.
- Our uniforms.
- Renovated the locker room.
- Our academic programs.

This is the time to make changes—when things are going well.

THE MENTOR PROGRAM

We have two mentor programs. The first is a program to help our incoming freshmen make the transition from high school to college. Each freshman gets assigned an upper-class mentor. We try to find a common theme between the mentor and mentee. For example, same position, same major, from the same high school, etc. The mentor meets with his mentee four times in the first semester. We even provided the agenda for each meeting. You can see our following mentor document. The mentor then reports the results to the coaching staff. This is a big part of our culture. It pulls the freshmen into the team and ensures a positive academic start.

Mission Statement:

The Ohio Wesleyan Men's Soccer Mentor Program is a program that is designed to provide guidance support and problem—solving assistance for the incoming student athlete. Academic, athletic, or social issues are all areas the mentor program is designed to address. The mentor(s) assigned to the incoming student athlete will help that student balance the newly found freedoms of college, with the many responsibilities that are also new. These mentors are successful student athletes at Ohio Wesleyan and can help the incoming student with problems and can assist him with finding any additional help and support he may need.

STUDENT ATHLETE:
MENTOR:

MENTOR PLAN:
PRESEASON MEETING

This meeting will address the following issues:

1. Student athlete and his mentor will go over his fall schedule. They will address any conflicts or concerns that athlete may have. At this time, the mentor will explain to the athlete what role they will play in his academic development.

2. The athlete and his mentor will discuss future plans and aspirations such as academic majors and minors.
3. The athlete and his mentor will discuss and examine his high school record, addressing any areas of concern and possible solutions, (scheduling, points of interest).

WEEK TWO MEETING

This meeting will be held after the first two weeks of the semester.

1. The athlete and his mentor will discuss classes and any concerns that they may have. They will also address any needed adds or drops to the athlete's schedule.
2. At this meeting, the mentor will contact all of the athlete's professors and set up a meeting with them. The mentor will explain the program to them and inform them of any conflicts due to the fall soccer schedule.
3. At this time, the athlete will give his mentor copies of his syllabi for each class.

MID-SEMESTER MEETING

1. The athlete and his mentor will discuss any concerns that the athlete or the mentor may have (academically, athletically, or socially) and develop a plan of action.
2. The athlete and his mentor will go over mid-term grades.
3. The athlete and his mentor will discuss class selection for the spring semester.

3/4 SEMESTER MEETING

1. Chart exam schedule.
2. Set up exam study schedule.
3. Approximate final averages.
4. Meet with professors if necessary.

OTHER ASPECTS

1. The mentor will also serve the athlete in other areas:
   - With regular exam preparation
     » With the writing process, introduction to the Writing Resource Center on campus and all it has to offer the athlete with the writing of papers and other course requirements.
     » Mentors will work closely with the athlete to help with all academic, soccer, and social adjustments.

DURATION

The mentor program will last for the athlete's first full year at Ohio Wesleyan. The second mentor program is the alumni mentor program. This program is aimed at the juniors and seniors as they prepare to leave OWU into the real world. We solicit alums to ask if they may be interested in this program. The response is typically overwhelming. We identify an alum in the same profession that the player is interested in pursuing. The alum will:

- Introduce himself to the player.
- Schedule meetings/phone calls to continue the conversation.
- Help "clean-up" the resume.
- Help securing internships. Often the alum will sponsor an internship at his firm.
- Help create a network for the player.
- Help with the final step of getting a job or going to grad school.

Both programs are popular and are a very important part of the culture.

SUMMER SCHOOL

Team dynamics is about putting a team together. Team cohesion is keeping the team together and performing at a high level for the whole season. This book is about team culture. Team culture plays a big role in both team dynamics and team cohesion.

As mentioned before, changing a group into a team is a four-part process:

- Forming: The team comes together. This is called preseason. There are very few problems at this time.
- Storming: As players jockey for a position on the team, problems can develop. I believe very few teams get through this stage!
- Norming: Pettiness is over and the players begin to accept their roles.
- Performing: Peak performance demands that a team go through this process.

The more you do in the forming stage to build culture, the better chance you have of getting through storming! We start the "culture process" early. We start the culture process in the summer. Starting June 1st, the players receive two emails a week from the coaching staff. The emails focus on the mental and the culture. Many of these emails have some "homework" that must be completed and returned within a set time period. This is important for all the players but really important for the incoming group. Setting the standards and expectations early, before the freshmen arrive on campus, is important. Here are some examples of the "summer school handouts":

Why We Do What We Do—Philosophy.
The Complete Player—Expectations.
Seven Ways to Build Real Self-Confidence—The Mental.
Ten Characteristics of a Champion—The Mental.
Training Habits—Expectations.
Dealing With Adversity—The Mental.
Controlling the Controllables—The Mental.
Controlling Emotions—The Mental.

When the players arrive on campus, we show a PowerPoint presentation that summarizes expectations, roles, philosophy, etc. It is the first thing we do after arrival. It is a summary of all the summer "homework." There is a new PowerPoint presentation every year.

MENTAL TRAINING IN PRACTICE

We expect every player to work on the mental side in practice just like they work on fitness, technique, and tactics. Players can not just "switch on" mental toughness. Like fitness, the players have to work on it. Here are the guidelines for mental training in practice:

- Get the most out of practice: Enjoy the chance to practice. View all the hard work that you do as an investment in yourself and the team. Working hard increases confidence.
- Devise a pre-practice routine: Design a routine that gets you 100 percent prepared for practice. Leave your concerns and problems in the locker room.
- Create a physical and mental mission to focus on before each practice: Decide on one or two goals for yourself for practice. One should be a physical goal and one should be a mental goal. You should work on each of these in practice.
- "Goal Dares": Have a teammate or a coach challenge you to improve in one area. i.e., Can you juggle 20 times without the ball hitting the ground?
- Challenge yourself on each activity: Don't go through the motions! Make every touch the best you can make it! Challenge yourself physically and mentally in every activity.
- Focused stretching: Use the stretching and warm-up time to get mentally prepared for the practice.
- Use and perfect a performance checklist: Discipline yourself to mentally run through your performance checklist every time you perform—not just games! Get mentally ready, have a plan, trust yourself, and evaluate your progress.

- Simulate competition: Practice like you compete. Go through every activity as if it were a game. Develop the habit necessary to compete at a higher level.

- Practice handling mistakes and adversity: Practices are filled with mistakes and problems. By perfecting your routines to handle adversity in practice, they will be automatic in games.

- Use down time to visualize: Use time in lines or between activities to visualize how you will correct mistakes.

- Use productive and positive self-talk: Stop a negative thought with a cue word and replace it with a positive thought. Do it. Make it a habit.

- Two-minute drill: If you are having problems in practice, focus on the next two minutes and then the next two minutes until things are going better. This works in games too.

- Evaluate: After each practice (and game) evaluate yourself. That is how you get better.

- Play with perspective: While soccer is important, remember and appreciate the other important aspects of your life: family, friends, academics, etc.) Playing with perspective helps you enjoy playing.

- Have fun: You started playing this game because it was fun—you have gone back to every practice because it is fun, don't stop having fun!

GIVING FEEDBACK

This is what coaches do! Feedback should help players move from where they are to where they want to be.

Jeff Janssen of the Janssen Sports Leadership Center suggests the following regarding feedback:

> Successful coaching depends on your feedback to motivate, challenge, direct, and support players on the quest to improve their skills.

The essence of coaching lies in your ability to develop an athlete and team so that they can reach their fullest potential. Regardless of a player's present level of ability, successful coaching depends on your feedback to motivate, challenge, direct and support players on the quest to improve their skills.

The quantity and especially the quality of feedback you give your players is one of the biggest keys to how well you can develop them. Giving effective feedback is an important communication skill for coaches. While every person responds a bit differently to coaching, there are some general principles that you can use when giving feedback to your players. In an effort to enhance your coaching, keep the following guidelines in mind as you and your players communicate with each other. The guidelines will help you create and maintain a positive and productive team environment.

1. POSITIVE

Many of the most successful coaches give much more positive, instructional-based feedback than negative. A study of famed basketball coach John Wooden found that, during a typical practice, he gave a ratio of three positive, instructional messages ("keep your knees bent, way to use a bounce pass, run the shuffle cut") to every one negative message ("that's a terrible shot"). Stop and consider what your ratio of positive, instructional to negative feedback might be. Is your ratio closer to 3:1 or 1:3? To better assess your coaching, you might want to have an observer watch a practice (without you knowing which one) and keep track of the quantity and quality of feedback you give. Or discuss with your staff the content of your feedback. Be sure to not only monitor the words you are saying but also the nonverbal messages you are sending your players. Many coaches are surprised at both the quantity and quality of feedback that they give during a typical practice. As management guru Ken Blanchard says, it's better to "catch people doing something right," than it is to only notice when they are doing something wrong.

2. SPECIFIC

The feedback you give should be as specific as possible. For example, instead of saying, "good job" in a general way, tell the player specifically what she did well. "Michelle, good job on keeping your head and glove down on that hard-hit ground ball" is a much more specific way of giving feedback. Be sure your players know exactly what you are praising them for and they will be more likely to repeat it.

3. SOON AFTER

Give your feedback as soon after the behavior or situation occurs as possible. If a player does something well, tell her right away instead of waiting until after practice (or a week later). The best example I can think of to illustrate this point is trying to train your dog to sit. When the dog begins to sit back on his hind legs, you need to immediately give him a doggie treat or a pat on the head. You can't train a dog to sit by waiting to reward it a day later. It's the same thing with humans. Praise them soon after they behave the way you want and reward them with a compliment.

4. FREQUENTLY WHILE LEARNING, LESS OFTEN WHEN MASTERED

Use both positive and corrective feedback often when players are first learning skills and strategies. The early and frequent feedback will help to build their confidence when they succeed and will get them back on track if they are struggling or off course. Then as the skills and strategies become better learned and mastered, less feedback is needed. This point is especially important for youth coaches since your players are very much in the learning stages of the game.

5. SINCERE

Be sure that your feedback is sincere because insincere feedback will end up backfiring on you. I once had a college coach who wanted to work on giving more praise to his players after discovering he had a 1:3 positive-to-negative ratio. While he did increase the quantity of his praise, the quality of his feedback left much to be desired. It seemed like he was saying "Good job" just to say it. His attempts to add more praise, while well-intentioned, actually hurt more than it helped. The players quickly sensed that his words were hollow and insincere. Thus, make sure that your feedback is honest and sincere.

6. ACKNOWLEDGE THE EFFORT, NOT JUST THE RESULTS

Finally, be sure to offer feedback for a player's effort, even if she is not successful. Sometimes your players will do all the right things but they will not get the desired result. However, they still need to be rewarded for the effort shown. For example, "Lauren that was a great effort you made diving for the ball on that play. Even though you didn't make the catch in that situation, you showed great aggressiveness." By praising the player for her effort despite not making the play, she will be more likely to maintain her aggressiveness giving her a better chance of making the next one.

The feedback you give as a coach is critical to taking your players and team to the next level. Look over the six guidelines again and ask your staff to rate how well you do each one of them. Determine each other's strengths and areas for improvement and then set a plan to enhance your coaching. Use your own coaching staff to coach you as you improve the quantity and quality of the feedback you give. Just as it is important for your players to develop and improve, so too must you invest some time into developing yourself as a coach.

PREPARING FOR THE BIG GAME

I am happy to report that we play in a lot of big games. We have won the conference 26+ times and been to 42 NCAA tournaments. When I was a young coach and we made our first NCAA tournament, the basketball coach at OWU gave me some advice I have never forgotten, *"You have to dance with who you brung!"* Meaning, don't make a lot of changes. The players will know it is a big game. You don't have to remind them.

Here is my advice about playing in a big game.

Do:

- Maintain a regular training program.
- Spend time each day thinking and rehearsing how you want to play.
- Prepare yourself mentally and physically for anything that may happen in the game . . . be prepared, never surprised . . . no panic . . . respond intelligently.
- Help yourself achieve a physical and mental high for the big game by using positive thoughts.
- Get the positive energy going with enthusiasm, positivity, eagerness, and confidence . . . become an avalanche of positive energy.
- Dress to win . . . adhere to all personal superstitions and rituals.
- Have fun and enjoy yourself during the big game. Think:
  - » I will give 100% effort all the time.
  - » I will be positive and optimistic.
  - » I will stay calm, relaxed, and confident.
  - » I will perform well.

Don't:

- Change your routine.
- Wait until the day before to begin thinking about the game.
- Make major changes in physical skills . . . keep it automatic.
- Get involved with personal problems or conflicts . . . no fights, bad movies, etc.
- Get anxious about feeling anxious. Being nervous is natural!
- Eat within 3 hours of game time.

Focus on the Moment . . . the Precious Present . . . the Next Play.

AVERTING THE FLAT PERFORMANCE

We have all had a game where the team comes out flat. I often wonder why? We only play a limited number of games. Why not get ready to play every one? Here are some tips to help avert a flat performance.

Getting Up for the Game:

- Means becoming energized and ready to play.
- Great athletes set a standard of personal expectation even for "lesser" games."
- What to do:
  - » Look forward to every game.
  - » Remember why you play—fun, enjoyment.
  - » Look forward to the challenge and opportunity.
  - » Be determined to play your best—do not worry about the outcome!
  - » Review your role and job in your mind—focus.
  - » Focus on the positive.
  - » Get into your pre-game routine.
  - » When the whistle blows GO AFTER *IT!*

Momentum As a Positive Energy Flow:

- Positive momentum = confidence, optimism, energy, alert.
- Negative momentum = lose focus, tired, feel game is over, etc.
- Momentum key: Forget external events and focus on NOW. What is happening to you NOW? What is your job?
- Most games have changes in momentum. When we lose momentum, we play two-touch and defend. When we get back in rhythm, we regain momentum.
- When our opponents have momentum, we must stay patient, poised, and fight to get momentum back.

The key to controlling momentum is controlling your own mental state, infusing yourself with positive energy and positive thought . . . controlling the internal and forgetting the external.

Individual Momentum

- A loss of momentum is usually a loss of focus. Get focus back!
- Have a cue word to "snap you back into NOW"!
- Use positive self-talk. Soccer is a negative game. Find the positive.

Team Momentum

- As a team, you must recognize the loss of momentum . . . ball chasing, only defending, can't put two passes together, players yelling at each other, etc.
- Retreat into the defensive half of the field.
- Get into our "defensive shape."
- Keep the ball in front of you.
- Pressure the ball hard and win it back.
- When we win it, keep it.
- Play two-touch until we get a rhythm.
- Attack the goal!

CONCLUSION

This book is not about soccer. It is not about coaching soccer. It is about coaching. Any coach of any sport can use the concepts and strategies in this book. The lessons in this book are a culmination of almost 50 years of coaching!

Much of the information shared comes from me. It includes strategies that have evolved over a long period of time. These strategies work. Look at the record coaching two sports at OWU. Some strategies come from others. I cited those in the book and in the bibliography.

When I share some of these strategies with coaches in a coaching clinic setting, the first question is always, "Jay these are great. But doesn't it take a long time?" My response is always, "Yes, it does. How much do you enjoy winning?" These concepts do take time. But it is your job to help your players grow as humans. A single soccer game does not matter.

The basic philosophy of Ohio Wesleyan soccer is that of building relationships and empowering the athletes. The problem is that many coaches are afraid of giving up "power." I don't know why. At the previously mentioned clinics, I tell the coaches, "To gain more *power*, you have to give up *power!*" What happens when you give up power? You immediately gain more trust and credibility with the players.

I think that trust and credibility are two of the most important characteristics of a successful coach. Both are hard to develop and so easy to lose. By empowering your players, trust will prevail.

I have had many Division I soccer coaches tell me that "all this is nice, but it won't work in DI. We must win!" Well, I certainly don't have to win to keep my job. I am a tenured professor. But the truth is we have won more games than any coach in any division! We want to win too. In fact, it is insulting to me that the DI guys even think that. What about Coach K? Pete Carrol?

Steve Kerr? Greg Popovich? And more. They all "have to win." They just do it differently than most coaches.

I am asked often. "What is the best thing about your program?" The answer? "Every Mother's Day when I see all of our seniors graduate!" And it's true. Our graduation rate is over 95 percent in 45 years.

Try out these strategies. Put in some time. You will reap the benefits. Please feel free to contact me with questions and comments.

Email: jamartin@owu.edu
Phone: 614-204-3975

Thank you!

APPENDIX A
MARTIN'S DEFINITION
OF GOOD SOCCER
AND A GOOD PLAYER

OHIO WESLEYAN UNIVERSITY SOCCER 2022

What Is Good Soccer?

Good Soccer	Bad Soccer
1. Play on ground.	Played in the air.
2. Ball control and accurate.	Played first time.
3. Frequent and accurate shots.	Rare opportunities.
4. Shots come from skillfully created openings.	Shots come from rebounds and errors.
5. Players vary passing and dribbling.	Players pass and kick hopefully.
6. Players make space.	Players create no time or space.
7. Players have purpose.	No purpose or aim.
8. Players change position.	No movement.
9. Players use skill.	Players foul and intimidate.

10. Defenders mark, cover and tackle fairly.	Late hits, yellow cards and violent tackles.
11. Players play for each other.	Players play for themselves.
12. Players use positive communication.	Players whine and curse.
13. Players come off the field physically exhausted.	Players come off the field A with something left.
14. Players are confident.	Players are afraid to make mistakes.
15. Players make good and quick decisions.	Players are slow with decision Making.
16. Players are creative.	Players are predictable.
17. Players want to get better.	Players are content with their level of play.
18. Players have fun.	The game becomes work.

What Is a Quality Player?

1. A definition:
   - You have sensitive touch and tight control . . . can receive the ball under pressure.
   - Can you make space/time for yourself?
   - Are you deceptive?
   - Can you get "out of trouble?"
   - Can you combine with a player? With a third player?

2. Does the player "have a game?"
   - Do you play for yourself or for others? Can you do both if necessary?
   - Do you create problems without the ball?
   - Can you free yourself from tight markers? Can you free others?
   - Do you react to play or are you a move or two ahead of the play?
   - Are you farsighted or nearsighted?

3. What are the physical attributes?
   - Do you have fluid movement?
   - Do you have good agility?
   - Do you have a good change of pace?
   - Can you produce a high level of work and sustain it over time?
   - Do you use athletic ability or do you depend upon it?
   - Are you strong in 1v1 situations?

4. What kind of competitor are you?
   - Can you impose your will on opponents?
   - How do you react to intimidation?
   - How do you react to dirty play?
   - Do you have physical and moral courage?
   - How tough minded are you?
   - How do you react to losing?

APPENDIX B
OWU PLAYER EVALUATION I

This is the first page of the player evaluation. This is used for all players except goalkeepers. The player evaluates himself. And the coach evaluates the player. There is a meeting between the coach and player to agree on the evaluation.

OWU PLAYER EVALUATION 2022

Date _____

Rated 1 to 5 (1 = excellent, 5 = poor)

Mental:

Coachability   _____
Desire to improve   _____
Commitment to the program   _____
Maturity   _____
Dealing with adversity   _____
1v1—winning the duel   _____
Ability to concentrate   _____
Leadership   _____

Physical:

Quickness   _____
Speed   _____
Strength   _____
Endurance   _____
Explosiveness (change of pace)   _____
Athleticism   _____

Technical:

Maintaining possession   _____
Dribbling to beat opponent   _____
Dribbling for speed   _____
Shielding   _____
Receiving balls on the move   _____
First touch   _____
Inside of foot passes   _____
Driven balls   _____
Deception   _____
Shooting threat   _____
Heading   _____
Ability to combine   _____

APPENDIX C
OWU PLAYER EVALUATION II

This is part II of the player evaluation. This is position-specific, and the focus is on attacking and defending.

CENTRAL MIDFIELDER

Defending:

1v1   _____
Covering   _____
Providing balance (weak side)   _____
Positioning   _____
Ball-winning   _____
Tackling   _____
Heading   _____
Commitment until regained possession   _____
Work rate   _____

Attacking:

Support play of backs   _____
Support play of forwards/midfielders   _____
Delivery of the ball to dangerous position   _____
Maintaining possession   _____
Combining with teammates   _____
Running at goal   _____
Heading   _____
Long-range shooting threat   _____
Ability to cover ground   _____
Changing the point of attack   _____

FORWARD

Defending:

1v1   _____
Shepherding   _____
Positioning   _____
Ball-winning   _____
Commitment until regained possession   _____
Work rate   _____

Attacking:

1v1 to beat defender   _____
Runs to receive the ball back   _____
Runs to receive the ball behind the defense   _____
Ability to hold the ball under pressure   _____
Combining with teammates to penetrate   _____
Shooting threat   _____
Heading to score   _____
Volleys   _____
Making space for teammates   _____
Crossing the ball   _____
Creating danger for opponents   _____

WING MIDFIELDER

Defending:

1v1   _____
Covering   _____
Providing balance (weak side)   _____
Positioning   _____
Ball-winning   _____
Tackling   _____
Heading   _____
Commitment until regained possession   _____
Work rate   _____

Attacking:

1v1 to beat defender   _____
Combining to beat defender   _____
Support play for backs   _____
Support play for forwards   _____
Support play for central midfielders   _____
Providing dangerous serves   _____
Decision making   _____
Attacking centrally   _____
Scoring threat   _____
Spinning away from pressure to possess   _____
Getting on the end of crosses   _____
Ability to cover ground   _____

Defending:

Marking a man ⎯⎯⎯

Denying the ball ⎯⎯⎯

Approach ⎯⎯⎯

Control/Restraint ⎯⎯⎯

Preventing the pass/shot ⎯⎯⎯

Jockeying ⎯⎯⎯

Tackling ⎯⎯⎯

Covering ⎯⎯⎯

Providing balance (weak side) ⎯⎯⎯

Positioning ⎯⎯⎯

Heading ⎯⎯⎯

Communication ⎯⎯⎯

Intimidation ⎯⎯⎯

Attacking:

Penetrating passes to midfielders ⎯⎯⎯

Penetrating passes to forwards' feet ⎯⎯⎯

Penetrating passes over the top ⎯⎯⎯

Running with the ball ⎯⎯⎯

Dangerous services ⎯⎯⎯

Ability to keep possession ⎯⎯⎯

Supporting runs ⎯⎯⎯

Ability to attack ⎯⎯⎯

APPENDIX D
THE MOTIVATION BY OBJECTIVES WORKSHEET

OHIO WESLEYAN UNIVERSITY 2022

Name:

What are your **strengths** as a player?

What are your **weaknesses** as a player?

S	**Specific**
M	**Measurable**
A	**Attainable**
R	**Realistic**
T	**Timeline**

What are your **personal** goals as a player?

Goal 1:

Goal 2:

Goal 3:

Goal 4:

As a result of the above list, **what is your plan?**

What are your **personal goals** as a student?

Goal 1:

Goal 2:

Goal 3:

Goal 4:

As a result of the above list, **what is your plan?**

What are your **personal goals** as a person?

Goal 1:

Goal 2:

Goal 3:

Goal 4:

As a result of that above list, **what is your plan?**

APPENDIX E
GAME GOALS

This is given to the players at the practice before each game. It is to be completed and returned to the coaching staff before the game.

OWU vs. Wabash

Game #12

Please list your goal(s) for the game. Try to identify the potential obstacles that may deter you from reaching the goal(s). Decide what your *Personal Action Plan* for the game will be and write it down.

Goals . . .	Potential	Obstacles	Personal Action Plan	Evaluation

Big NCAC Game!

BIBLIOGRAPHY

Angel, Ben, *Unstoppable*, Irvine California, Entrepreneur Press, 2018.

Beswick, Bill, *ONE GOAL: The Mindset of Winning Soccer Teams*, Champaign IL, Human Kinetics, 2016.

Carroll, Pete, *Live, Work, and Play Like a Champion*, New York, New York, Penguin Books, 2010.

Covey, Stephen, *Principle-Centered Leadership*, New York, New York, First Fireside Edition, 1992.

Connolly, Fergus, *Game Changer*, Canada, Victory Belt Publishing Co, 2017.

Coyle, Daniel, *The Talent Code*, New York, New York Bantam Dell, 2009.

Coyle, Daniel, *The Culture Code*, New York, New York, Bantam Books, 2018.

Davis, Seth, *Getting to Us*, New York, New York, Penguin Press, 2018.

Epstein, David, *The Sports Gene*, New York, New York, The Penguin Group, 2013.

Epstein, David, *Range: Why Generalists Triumph in a Specialized World,* New York, Riverhead Books, 2019.

Evans, Ceri, *Perform Under Pressure,* Auckland, NZ, Harper Collins Publisher, 2019.

Garfield, Charles, *Peak Performance*, New York, New York, William Morrow and Company, 1986.

Gilbert, Wade, *Coaching Better Every Season*, Champaign, IL, Human Kinetics, 2017.

Kerr, James, *Legacy*, Great Britain, Constable Printers, 2013.

Kidman, Lynn, *Developing Decision Makers*, Christchurch, New Zealand, Innovative Print Communications Ltd, 2001.

Krzysewski, Mike, *The Gold Standard*, New York, New York, Hachette Book Group, 2009.

Lemov, Doug, *Practice Perfect*, San Francisco, CA, Jossey-Bass, 2012.

Lemov, Doug, *The Coach's Guide to Teaching,* Woodbridge UK, John Catt Educational Ltd, 2020.

Lencioni, Patrick, *Leadership Fables: The Five Dysfunctions of a Team*, San Francisco, CA, Jossey-Bass 2005.

Loehr, James, *Mental Toughness Training for Sports,* Denver, CO, Forum Publishing Co, 1985.

Mairs, Paul, *Coaching Outside the Box*, Syracuse, NY, Mairs & Shaw Publishing, 2012.

Otte, Paul, *We Leadership*, Columbus, Ohio, Paul Otte and Ross Leadership Institute, 2011.

Ungerleider, Steve, *Mental Training for PEAK Performance*, United States, Rodale Inc., 2005.

Walker, Sam, *The Captain Class*, New York New York, Random House, 2017.

Walsh, Bill, *The SCORE Takes Care of Itself*, New York, New York, Penguin Books, 2010.

Whitaker, Nathan, Dungy, Tony, *The Mentor Leader*, Winter Park, FL, Tyndale House Publishers Inc., 2010.

Williams, Mark and Wigmore, Tim, *The Best: How Elite Athletes are Made,* Boston, Nicholas Brealey Publishing, 2020.

Willink, Jocko and Babin, Leif, *Extreme Ownership: How Navy Seals Lead and Win,* New York, St. Martin's Press, 2015.

ABOUT THE AUTHOR

How broad is Ohio Wesleyan head coach **Jay Martin's** record of service to soccer? Come up with any combination of level (high school, college, professional) and function (player, coach, administrator), and he's probably done it. Martin is the winningest coach in NCAA men's soccer history with a total of 738 wins. He is the first men's soccer coach in any NCAA division to reach the 700-win mark.

Heading into the 2022 season, he guided his 44 Battling Bishop soccer teams to a 738-153-76 record. His career winning percentage of .802 entering the 2022 season ranks 12th all-time in the NCAA. In 2021, the Bishops finished second in the North Coast Athletic Conference championship race with a 8-1-0 record and advanced to the second round of the NCAA Division III tournament on the way to a 15-3-2 overall mark. In 44 seasons, Martin's teams have compiled a 291-30-22 record in conference play, a winning percentage of .880, and have won 26 conference crowns.

In 2011, Martin guided Ohio Wesleyan to its second NCAA Division III national championship. Along the way, the Bishops extended their unbeaten string in NCAC competition to a league-record 40 games. Another peak in Martin's already illustrious coaching career came when he guided the Battling Bishops to the 1998 NCAA Division III championship.

His teams have reached the NCAA Division III semifinals nine times, finishing as national runner-up twice in addition to the 1998 and 2011 titles. They have been among the final 16 teams a total of 29 times and have brought home 12 regional titles, including 9 in the last 15 seasons that the NCAA tournament included a regional format. Ohio Wesleyan holds the NCAA Division III record with 42 playoff appearances and has recorded 65 playoff victories.

Martin's teams set another NCAA record with 18 consecutive Division III tournament berths from 1978-95 and have won an unprecedented 23 Stu Parry Awards, the latter recognizing Ohio's top Division III team each year.

He has been the NCAA Regional Coach of the Year 16 times in his 44 years at Ohio Wesleyan and was named NSCAA national Coach of the Year in 1991, 1998, and 2011. In 2000, Martin received the Ohio Collegiate Soccer Association's Honor Award, only the fourth time that award was bestowed since the association's founding in 1949. He received the National Soccer Coaches Association of America's Honor Award in 2007 and was inducted into the United Soccer Coaches Hall of Fame in 2020.

Under Martin's guidance, Ohio Wesleyan was the winningest men's soccer team in the NCAA—regardless of division—during the 1980s, compiling a winning percentage of .815 to top such programs as Indiana, UNC-Greensboro, and UCLA. The Battling Bishops bettered that during the 1990s, compiling a winning percentage of .825, and improved upon that during the 2000s, with a winning percentage of .827.

His lacrosse teams posted an 8-year record of 104-34, winning 3 Midwest Lacrosse Association titles, earning 6 NCAA playoff bids, and twice making Martin the MLA Coach of the Year. In both sports, in 51 seasons, Martin has turned out 61 All-America and 214 all-region or All-Midwest players.

Martin calls having fun the key. You have to have fun to do your best, and it helps to do so against the best competition. Hence, the Bishops' perennially ambitious schedules, liberally sprinkled with nationally-ranked opponents. He favors a skillful, ball-control games and rates his players as first-class athletes and men.

Beyond coaching, Martin also has served soccer with a term as president of the National Soccer Coaches Association of America as well as a six-year stint on the NCAA Division III selection committee, including four years as committee chair. He has been a color analyst of the Major League Soccer's Columbus Crew for nine seasons. In addition, he took over as editor of the NSCAA's *The Soccer Journal* in January 2003, becoming the publication's third editor since its establishment in 1950.

Martin is a professor in Ohio Wesleyan's Physical Education department. He served as the Battling Bishops' athletics director from 1985–2004. During his 19 years as athletics director, Ohio Wesleyan intercollegiate athletics enjoyed unprecedented success. Ohio Wesleyan won a conference-record six consecutive NCAC all-sports championships from 1988-94. More recently, the Battling Bishops finished in the top 25 of the NACDA Directors Cup NCAA Division III standings in six of the last eight academic years under Martin's leadership.

Prior to joining the Ohio Wesleyan faculty, Martin served as a two-sport assistant at Ohio State University, from which he received both MA and PhD degrees. Earlier, he was director of sport at the Munich, Germany, YMCA, coaching soccer, volleyball, basketball, and lacrosse. He was also athletics director at the American International School at Düsseldorf.

A native of Hingham, MA, Martin received his bachelor of arts from Springfield College in 1971. He lettered in soccer and lacrosse, earning All-America laurels in the latter. In Germany, he also played soccer for the Kaiserwerth Club, played professional basketball, and served on the staff of the Volleyball Pavilion at the 1972 Olympics.

Martin's Career Coaching Record

1977	Ohio Wesleyan	7-4-3	.607
1978	Ohio Wesleyan	11-5-2	.667
1979	Ohio Wesleyan	16-3-2	.810
1980	Ohio Wesleyan	16-4-1	.786
1981	Ohio Wesleyan	17-4-4	.760
1982	Ohio Wesleyan	17-2-3	.841
1983	Ohio Wesleyan	16-5-1	.750
1984	Ohio Wesleyan	15-4-1	.775
1985	Ohio Wesleyan	15-4-1	.775
1986	Ohio Wesleyan	20-3-0	.870
1987	Ohio Wesleyan	19-4-0	.826
1988	Ohio Wesleyan	17-1-3	.881
1989	Ohio Wesleyan	19-2-1	.886
1990	Ohio Wesleyan	20-4-1	.820
1991	Ohio Wesleyan	22-2-0	.917
1992	Ohio Wesleyan	20-4-0	.833
1993	Ohio Wesleyan	18-2-1	.881
1994	Ohio Wesleyan	20-0-1	.976
1995	Ohio Wesleyan	17-2-3	.841
1996	Ohio Wesleyan	13-4-2	.737
1997	Ohio Wesleyan	16-8-0	.667
1998	Ohio Wesleyan	18-6-0	.750
1999	Ohio Wesleyan	18-3-1	.841
2000	Ohio Wesleyan	23-1-0	.958
2001	Ohio Wesleyan	19-6-1	.750
2002	Ohio Wesleyan	18-4-1	.804
2003	Ohio Wesleyan	17-4-1	.795
2004	Ohio Wesleyan	16-2-2	.850
2005	Ohio Wesleyan	20-1-0	.952
2006	Ohio Wesleyan	15-1-6	.818

2007	Ohio Wesleyan	15-5-2	.727
2008	Ohio Wesleyan	18-5-1	.771
2009	Ohio Wesleyan	18-2-2	.864
2010	Ohio Wesleyan	19-2-2	.870
2011	Ohio Wesleyan	23-2-0	.920
2012	Ohio Wesleyan	13-3-5	.738
2013	Ohio Wesleyan	19-1-3	.891
2014	Ohio Wesleyan	17-5-4	.731
2015	Ohio Wesleyan	16-5-2	.739
2016	Ohio Wesleyan	10-5-3	.639
2017	Ohio Wesleyan	12-7-2	.619
2018	Ohio Wesleyan	13-4-2	.737
2019	Ohio Wesleyan	15-5-4	.708
2020	Ohio Wesleyan	season canceled	
2021	Ohio Wesleyan	15-3-2	.800
Career	**44 years**	**738-153-76**	**.802**

Credits

Cover and interior design: Anja Elsen

Layout: DiTech Publishing Services, www.ditechpubs.com

Interior images: Courtesy of Jay Martin

Managing editor: Elizabeth Evans

Copy editor: Sarah Tomblin, www.sarahtomblinediting.com